Banking in Virginia

SENATE OF VIRGINIA

SENATE JOINT RESOLUTION NO. 181

Commending the Virginia Bankers Association.

Patrons—Holland, R.J., Andrews, Barry, Bell, Benedetti, Calhoun, Chichester, Colgan, Cross, Earley, Gartlan, Goode, Hawkins, Holland, C.A., Holland, E.M., Houck, Howell, Lambert, Lucas, Marsh, Maxwell, Miller, K.G., Miller, Y.B., Nolen, Norment, Potts, Quayle, Reasor, Robb, Russell, Saslaw, Schewel, Stolle, Stosch, Trumbo, Waddell, Walker, Wampler and Woods

Agreed to by the Senate, January 21, 1993
Agreed to by the House of Delegates, January 25, 1993

WHEREAS, a sound banking system is essential to the economic growth and prosperity of the Commonwealth; and

WHEREAS, through the initiative and persistence of private citizens, Virginia's first bank, in Alexandria, was established by Act of the General Assembly on November 23, 1792; and

WHEREAS, over the past 201 years, Virginia's bankers have played a vital and continuing role in the establishment, growth, and success of the Commonwealth's farms, businesses, and communities; and

WHEREAS, almost a century ago, on October 11, 1893, Virginia's bankers met to organize the Virginia Bankers Association, which in 1993 celebrates its centennial anniversary; and

WHEREAS, over its 100 years of service to the citizens of the Commonwealth, the Virginia Bankers Association has furthered and enhanced the integral contribution of Virginia's bankers to the overall growth and prosperity of Virginia's economy; now, therefore, be it

RESOLVED by the Senate, the House of Delegates concurring, That the Virginia Bankers Association be hereby commended on the occasion of its centennial anniversary; and, be it

RESOLVED FURTHER, That the Clerk of the Senate prepare a copy of this resolution for presentation to the Virginia Bankers Association in recognition of its century of invaluable service to the Commonwealth and its citizens.

Susan Clarke Schaar
Clerk of the Senate

Banking in Virginia

By T. HARRY GATTON

T. Harry Gatton
June 21, 1993

This publication is part of the Centennial Observance
of the founding in 1893 of the Virginia Bankers Association.

Published by the Virginia Bankers Association
Richmond
1993

First Edition

Virginia Bankers Association
700 East Main Street
Richmond, Virginia 23219
Virginia

Library of Congress Catalogue Card Number 93-60091
International Standard Book Number 0-9636232-0-6

Manufactured in the United States of America

Contents

PART FIVE: Three Decades of Great Change—1900-1930

PART SIX: Depression and the Roosevelt Era

PART SEVEN: Market Forces and Financial Reform—1943-1993

PART EIGHT: VBA's First Century—Banking Changes and Benchmarks of an Organization

PART NINE: For the Record

Virginia Governor Douglas Wilder joined the Virginia General Assembly in calling recognition to the 100th Anniversary of the Virginia Bankers Association on February 13, 1993. In a special ceremony in the Governor's office, Governor Wilder officially presented the commending resolution earlier passed by the Assembly. He then signed a ceremonial check paid in the amount of 100 years to the Virginia Bankers Association for 100 years of service to Virginia. Shown above, left to right, are Doug Monroe, Paul Geithner, Vern Henley, Governor Wilder, Walter Ayers and Senator Richard Holland.

Doug Monroe, Paul Geithner, Senator Holland listen as Governor Wilder reads the wording on the check.

Governor Wilder signs check as Monroe, Geithner and Holland look on.

Preface

A historian friend has written that "The wheel of history turns on an axis of human achievement."

The study undertaken of the banking history of Virginia for the Virginia Bankers Association, quickly revealed an inseparable relationship between the VBA and banking for a century.

The study shows how contrasts often produced colorful leaders and diverse issues. This history is essentially anecdotal by design and often portrays the lighter side of people and issues. I do hope that the reader will see it as a valuable and readable source of information about banking in the Old Dominion. The total value of the contributions of banking to Virginia's development is phenomenal.

To acknowledge appropriately the remarkable cooperation from a broad spectrum of institutions and individuals who have provided information and help is not possible. No doors have been closed by these individuals, libraries, public archives, banks or private collections.

My particular gratitude goes to the Virginia Bankers Association, its officials, members, and highly professional staff headed by Walter C. Ayers. Mrs. Barbara Garrett did yeoman work as coordinator for the book. Joe Ward, chairman of the 100th Anniversay Task Force, developed a broad-based observance. Many thanks to my former superior colleagues in banking association management— Rawley F. Daniel, Marchant D. Wornom and W.O. (Wink) Pearce, predecessors of Walter Ayers. Lois R. Lee, now retired after 30 years with VBA, is a living memory source. The VBA has been fortunate through the years from Walter H. Taylor to Paul H. Geithner, Jr., and onward next to V.W. Henley, to benefit from the wise leadership of able Presidents.

A special word of appreciation to my wife, Mary, who helped me in research. At one time when we resided in Virginia she was on the staff of the late U.S. Senator A. Willis Robertson.

T. HARRY GATTON

The VBA's Annual Banquets featured impressive programs. Above is the cover of the 1919 program at the Hotel Chamberlin.

Introductory Note

Perhaps more than most, people of Virginia are imbued with an abiding sense of things historical. No doubt that fascination and appreciation of history arises, at least in part, from a justifiable pride in an ancestry that has contributed so much to what we know about ourselves as a nation. It was a natural progression in the scheme of things, then, when the Board of Directors of the Virginia Bankers Association, on the occasion of the Association's 100th Anniversary, commissioned the writing of Banking in Virginia.

In this entertaining, yet uniquely informative anecdotal history of Virginia banking, Harry Gatton adds yet another must-read treatise to the treasure chest of Virginia historical works. As is the case in the general affairs of government and people, Gatton documents that Virginia and Virginians have also been leaders in the banking industry. Indeed, in his book, developments in banking and developments in the general affairs of the Commonwealth frequently seem very much entwined. That is still true today.

In any historical work, significance can be found in the spectrum of developments from the beginning point to the concluding point. Such is the case in this work. Gatton reveals that the first president of the Virginia Bankers Association was a chief aide to Confederate General Robert E. Lee. One hundred years later, the Association starts its second hundred years with its first black president. It is a leap, but a leap that took 100 years. Much happens in between.

Those of us who are still making banking history, I believe, can draw guidance and inspiration from reading *Banking in Virginia.* It will simultaneously make us proud of the industry's heritage, and challenge us to measure up to those who were the leaders and giants of their day.

WALTER C. AYERS
Executive Vice President
Virginia Bankers Association

Virginia chartered its first bank on November 23, 1792, in Alexandria. The above sketch is from a 1974 published study by Architect J. Everette Fauber, Jr.

PART ONE

Banking—Virginia Beginnings

1

First State Chartered Bank—Bank of Alexandria—George Washington a Stockholder

"...well regulated banks are highly useful to society."
—Preamble from 1792 bill in Virginia General Assembly

THE STORY OF BANKING IS A SIGNIFICANT PART of the economic development of Virginia and the nation, development that would not have been possible without the credit and other services provided by banks.

The city of Alexandria was the home of Virginia's first bank. It was a busy seaport town on the Potomac River before Washington was established as the nation's seat of government and Alexandria was a strong rival of Baltimore and Norfolk for commerce. Peopled by an increasing number of prosperous merchants and other citizens, the city looked to the political arena for action.

In 1791, residents of Alexandria sought to secure a branch of the newly formed First Bank of the United States, a national bank promoted by Alexander Hamilton and the Federalists. That effort proved unsuccessful, however, as Norfolk turned out to be the only Virginia city selected for a branch, and that selection was not made until 1799.

Not to be denied, 125 Alexandria merchants drafted a petition and sent it to Richmond in October 1792. In the petition they asked for a charter for a bank with a capital of not less than $100,000. This was an unprecedented action in Virginia, although chartered banks already existed in Maryland. Since banks were looked upon with suspicion by a segment of colonial society, the Virginia applicants had to prepare their case well. This was experimental legislation— and many details were included to reassure the legislators that every effort would be made to justify approval as being in the public interest.

The proponents prevailed. The charter for the Bank of Alexandria was approved on November 23, 1792, as "An Act for establishing a Bank in the Town of Alexandria." It set a precedent for state chartering of banks in the Old Dominion.

The preamble to the 1792 bill clearly showed that a new day had arrived, one calculated to bolster the economy and to serve the people.

It declared: "WHEREAS, the experience of commercial nations for several ages past has fully evinced, that well-regulated banks are highly useful to society, by promoting punctuality in the performance of contracts, increasing the medium of trade, facilitating the payment of taxes, increasing the exportation of specie, furnishing for it a safe deposit, and by discount rendering easy and expeditious the anticipation of funds...."

Capital for the new bank—incorporated under the title of "President, Directors, and Company of the Bank of Alexandria"—was set at $150,000, to be subscribed in shares of $200 each, paid in installments, with only $10 in specie to be required at first.

George Washington was a stockholder in the Bank of Alexandria.
(Courtesy NC Archives)

The charter was set to expire on January 1, 1801. The rates for loans (discounts) was set at six percent, and no circulating notes were to be issued for less than five dollars.

Stock shares went on sale December 7, 1792, at the Alexandria Court House. The result was amazing. In less than two hours the whole number of shares was subscribed. On the list of prominent shareholders was President George Washington of nearby Mount Vernon.

The new bank purchased a building on Cameron Street between Fairfax and Royal, and opened for business on March 30, 1792. To serve the public the bank was open daily except Sundays and observed only two holidays, Christmas and the Fourth of July. Philip R. Fendel was the first president, Gurdin Chapin was the first cashier and there were two porters.

The death penalty awaited those who counterfeited the bank's notes. The circulating notes bore a dire warning that such crime was punishable by death "without benefit of clergy."

The death penalty awaited those who counterfeited the bank's notes.

Dividends paid on the capital stock were good. For example, the rate was four and one-half percent in 1795, and it jumped to eight and one-half percent in 1796. In 1807 the bank moved to Fairfax and Cameron Street, where it operated until it failed on April 12, 1834, a victim of President Andrew Jackson's veto of the charter extension of the Second Bank of the United States which led to the removal of funds from many banks.

The Bank of Alexandria proved to be a true pioneer. J. Everette Fauber, Jr., a Virginia architect, made a thorough study of the Bank of Alexandria in 1974, and his research included a review of the bank's records. In his published study he observed:

"As Alexandria grew from a warehouse town into a major seaport, the Bank of Alexandria played no small part in offering support to merchants, stability to the financial situation, and ready money for commerce. It contributed greatly to the growth of the prosperity of this seaport town. It may well be imagined that the banking house was a busy place, its floors tracked with street mud, that one could hear there the murmur of busy merchants, the backwoods drawl of farmers, and the occasional hearty laugh of a seaman. The town was a cosmopolitan place in the first of the nineteenth century. There were ships in the harbor from all over the world, and the shops were crowded with exotic imports. The streets were alive with farmers from the west, politicians from the new capital city just across the river, and sailors from the busy wharves. It was, no doubt, an exciting time for the town of Alexandria, and the Bank of Alexandria participated in and contributed to this general atmosphere of excitement, progress, and prosperity."

The second bank in Virginia was the Bank of Virginia. It was incorporated by the General Assembly on January 13, 1804, with a capital stock of $1,500,000, apportioned 3,750 shares to Richmond, 3,000 to Norfolk, 2,250 to Petersburg, 1,000 to Fredericksburg, 525 to Winchester, 430 to Staunton, and 525 to Lynchburg. The charter limited the total number of bank notes for circulation to $4,500,000.

According to John Jay Knox, in his *History of Banking,* the bank was highly successful. Its notes were paid in gold, had a wide circulation, and were at only one-fourth of one percent discount in New York. With its only competition in the state coming from the small local Bank of Alexandria and the branch of the First Bank of the United States at Norfolk, the Bank of Virginia gained great power between 1804 and 1812 and "enjoyed the banking monopoly of the state."

Banking historians point out that the early banking system resembled the Scottish system in that heavy capitalization was required. "The most distinctive feature of the system...was the wide extension of branch banking," wrote University of Virginia Professor George T. Starnes in his book *Sixty Years of Branch Banking in Virginia.* He concluded, "In no other state did the system of branch banking attain such a high state of development and receive such a thorough trial as in Virginia." He notes that prior to 1851, when independent banks became common, large mother banks with many branches constituted the only type of bank legally permitted to do business in Virginia. The explanation lies in the fact that smaller communities could not generate the capital required to establish a bank. Richmond, for example, had wanted a local bank for a long time, and the Bank of Virginia was the fulfillment of a need that had been recognized by the city's more prosperous merchants.

After much discussion, a second mother bank in Richmond—the Farmers Bank of Virginia—was approved on February 13, 1812, with a capital of $2,000,000. Provided in the charter were branches at Lynchburg, Winchester, Petersburg and Fredericksburg. The charter also provided that 3,334 shares of stock were to be given the state, paid for out of the half-yearly dividends of the bank.

The new bank had 15 directors and 13 for each of the branch banks at Lynchburg, Winchester, Petersburg and Fredericksburg. Nine directors were to be elected by the Legislature for the mother bank, and eight for each of the branch banks. The stockholders were to elect the remainder. Something new was added when each branch of the Farmers Bank was to issue its own circulating notes used for "functions necessary to meet the requirements of the community in which it was established." Note circulation was enhanced when the notes from the branch banks were traded with the mother bank in Richmond.

No reserve requirements were mandated of these early banks, and Knox noted, "they kept none except the specie held in their vaults to redeem their notes."

The business of banking and the issue of bills spawned a number of private or unchartered banks. As their notes became widely circulated—and frequently unredeemed—the General Assembly passed an act on February 24, 1816, that declared all unchartered banks illegal in Virginia. The legislation was a reaction to the fact that the state had no authority to regulate the unchartered banks or to control the circulation of their notes.

The first banks became profit centers.

The first banks became profit centers. More charter applications were developed. The Bank of the Valley of Winchester was established February 5, 1817. Another early bank was the Exchange Bank of Norfolk, which was established by special act on March 25, 1837, with authorized capital of more than three million dollars.

In his *History of Banking,* Knox characterized Virginia as having a very liberal for the Second Bank was reversed, coming from the South, with Northern opposition.

Said Senator William Bibb of Georgia, "The patient is sick from the crown of his head to the sole of his feet; he asks for oil and wine to be poured into his wounds, which would otherwise be fatal."

Senate passage took place by a vote of 23 to 10 on April 1, 1816, following approval by the House. President Madison signed the act into law on April 10, 1816. The charter for the Second Bank of the United States was for a duration of 20 years. The bank's headquarters were established in Philadelphia. Branches were authorized and capital was set at $20 million, with the Federal government to furnish 20 percent of the total. The bank was to be operated as a semi-private enterprise.

In short order 18 branches were approved. To reflect the growth of Virginia, two branches were established in the Old Dominion—one in Richmond, the other in Norfolk.

In 1817 tension increased between the Second Bank of the United States and the state-chartered institutions over resumption of specie payments. The Second Bank was obligated to enforce specie payments to help restore an orderly currency in the nation.

Under the leadership of another distinguished Virginia statesman, Chief Justice John Marshall, the United States Supreme Court spoke directly to the heart of the question of whether the Second Bank of the United States was constitutional. In 1819 in the case of *McCulloch vs. Maryland* the Court decided that the Second Bank was a proper and necessary instrument of the United States government in carrying out fiscal operations. In this famous case, the court found that Maryland's attempt to tax the bank's Baltimore branch was unconstitutional.

2

The Jackson "Bank War" Polarizes Politics

*"The Bank is trying to kill me,
but I will kill it."*
—Andrew Jackson, veto message of the act to renew the
charter of the Second Bank of the United States.

A POLITICAL "WAR" AGAINST THE SECOND BANK broke out after General Andrew Jackson was elected President in 1828.

Although the Bank had served as a fairly effective balance wheel for stability, Jackson was bitterly opposed to the Second Bank. He accused it of being a source of special privilege and great wealth to the stockholders. He charged that it gave

President Jackson's veto destroyed the Philadelphia Second Bank of the United States, including its branches in Richmond and Norfolk, causing a political furor in Virginia and the nation.
(Courtesy NC Archives)

too much power over the country's economic life to a few private individuals.

Jackson believed the Second Bank would destroy the state banks.

A Jackson supporter remarked that the Second Bank had "never raised a single bushel of wheat, nor even a single head of cabbage nor a single pumpkin, potato or turnip during its whole existence, nor never will."

At first, the Second National Bank had management difficulties, but its third and last president, Nicholas Biddle, was an able administrator. A member of a prominent Philadelphia family, Biddle had entered the University of Pennsylvania at age 10. Although he completed his course work in three years, he was refused a degree because of his youth. He overcame that setback by enrolling at Princeton, where he was graduated at age 15, the valedictorian of his class.

Jackson believed the Second Bank would destroy the state banks. His support came from several sources including some of the New York bankers who were jealous of Philadelphia's position as the nation's banking center at that time. Biddle was forced to use all his political clout to ward off the attacks from his growing list of opponents.

Even though he was an able manager and understood the fine points of banking, Biddle made a grave error in agreeing to a plan to request the Congress to renew the bank's charter in 1832, four years before such action was required. Henry Clay, who wished to succeed Jackson, and Daniel Webster, both powerful Senators, agreed with the plan in order to get a political "jump" on Jackson.

Jackson's hot temper rose to a boiling point, destroying all possibility of compromise, and dividing the nation in what was called the "Bank War." The presidential campaign of 1832 became a referendum on the bank's future.

Partisans took their political battle stations. Pro-Jackson editors wrote of the Second Bank, "We are shamefully prostrated at the feet of this Colossus.... Everything must be ground to dust under its pressure." The Second Bank, of course, had its friends, because to many it was a shield and sanctuary.

Petitions for and against the Bank poured in from Virginia and other states. In the midst of a mid-summer Washington heat wave the Senate approved the charter bill on June 11 by a vote of 28-20; the House voted favorably—107 to 85—on July 3. The act was sent to President Jackson. On July 10 he returned it unsigned. His veto message was hailed as a great victory for the anti-bank forces. Jackson's words were denounced by Biddle as "the rabble rousing cry of a deranged demagogue preaching anarchy."

Congress adjourned on July 16, unable to override the veto. Biddle continued to fume over the loss. Said he, "I am not a Whig. I am not a Locofoco. I once belonged to a party now obsolete called the Democratic Party, a very good party until it was spoiled by General Jackson. I am now only an American Citizen deeply concerned in the welfare and very anxious about the character of the country."

Jackson snatched the power from the Eastern dynasty in national affairs and transferred it to the most agrarian states. The upshot of the struggle was the emergence of the Whig Party.

Deposits from the Second Bank were transferred to widespread state banks, called "pet banks" by Jackson critics.

Jackson's veto also killed the possibility of a central bank until the Federal Reserve was created in 1913, with Virginians again in the leadership role.

Professor of History Robert V. Remini, University of Illinois, has written in his *Andrew Jackson and the Bank War:* "In abolishing one efficient central banking system, Jackson can be faulted for not substituting another: one better controlled but able to provide the country with adequate currency and credit. Some historians feel that his failure here condemned the nation to a century of unsound finance...."

He concluded that the Second Bank of the United States was caught between "two willful, proud, stubborn men."

3

Pre-Civil War Prosperity

"The period from 1834 to 1860 is referred to ... as 'The halcyon days when there was a bank at every cross roads.'"
John Knox, Bank Historian

THE OLD DOMINION'S BANKS HAVE BEEN SOUND, through thick and thin. With abundant natural resources, a balanced economy and a growing population, Virginians mounted major efforts in the early 1800s to build canals and railroads and improve roads and port facilities. Bankers financed many of these projects.

The Panic of 1837 slowed the pace of progress. Almost immediately upon President Martin Van Buren's inauguration that year, the country faced a major national depression, caused in part by the defiance by business of Jackson's hard money policy. Hard money—specie—was withdrawn from banks to take care of heavy speculation in Western lands. Almost all banks were forced to suspend specie payments. Commodity prices fell. The political result was Van Buren's defeat in the election of 1840. The next president was Virginia native William Henry Harrison, a Whig, who died in office one month after his inauguration in 1841. He was succeeded by Vice President John Tyler of Virginia, a former Democrat who had served as Governor of the Old Dominion and as a member of the U.S. House of Representatives and Senate. Tyler had switched to the Whig Party in 1836 and resigned his Senate seat.

The so-called Bank Panic of 1837 left anti-bank prejudices, continuing the banking controversy. The panic arose after President Jackson signed the Specie Circular on July 11, 1836, in an attempt to decrease wild speculation on land. The law stipulated that after August 15, 1836, all purchases of public land had to be paid in specie. A wild scramble for specie ensued, causing a panic among those engaged in buying land.

In 1838 Virginia enacted a law for another system of banks—deposit and discount banks. They became very numerous because they had few restrictions, they operated under what was described as the "go-as-you-please" plan. Directors were given wide authority in running the bank. Failure to pay depositors on demand carried a strong penalty of 10 percent on the whole amount from the time of failure until payment was made.

The Commercial Savings Bank, Richmond, chartered in 1853, was an institution of this class. Organized by 15 businessmen who were owners and directors, each gave a note for $2,500, and paid it down at the rate of $50 per month. No dividends were declared. Profits were accumulated. No person could borrow money without one of the owners as endorser.

Virginia banks from 1837 to 1860 were prosperous. An average of $10 million of note circulation was reported with no losses. The Panic of 1837 forced these banks to suspend specie payments, but they managed to survive. The Virginia Assembly required them to resume specie payments on May 1, 1858. They complied, and continued until the onset of the Civil War. On January 1, 1860, there were 24 banks of circulation with 41 branches in Virginia.

Resources and liabilities of these banks were given as:

RESOURCES		LIABILITIES	
Loans and discounts	$24,975,792	Capital	$16,005,156
Stocks	3,584,079	Circulation	9,812,197
Real estate	1,019,032	Deposits	7,729,652
Other investments	433,423	Due other banks	1,138,327
Due by other banks	2,756,047	Other liabilities	34,600
Cash items	29,838		
Notes of other banks	1,294,093		
Specie	2,943,652		

The Civil War ended the most prosperous period of Virginia banking.

The Civil War era ended the most prosperous period of Virginia banking. The declaration of war between the North and South derailed Virginia's efforts for reconciliation, urged by John Tyler and others. After it was clear that these efforts had failed, Tyler asked, "Whither are you going? You have to choose your association. Will you find it among the icebergs of the North or the cotton fields of the South?" The Virginia Peace Commission in 1861 adopted an ordinance of secession on a vote of 103-46, with some of the negative votes coming from counties that in 1863 would become West Virginia. Voters of the Commonwealth ratified the ordinance of secession on May 23, 1861, by a vote of 125,950 to 20,373, a six-to-one majority. The convention had previously elected the venerable Tyler as one of five representatives to the Confederate Congress.

In every respect—including banking—Virginia now faced great sacrifice and change.

PART THREE

War and Recovery

1

The Confederacy and Banking

"The shock of the Civil War provided the stimulus for change."
—Paul B. Trescott, *Financing American Enterprise*

WAR CAME TO THE OLD DOMINION IN 1861. After significant reluctance to leave the Union, the decision had been made on May 23.

Richmond banker William H. Macfarland, former lieutenant governor, president of the Farmers Bank, railroad and civic promoter, active in "the whole life of the community," sought to prevent the national split.

The banker was elected as a Union delegate to the Richmond convention which met in February 1861, but shortly thereafter cast his lot with the Confederacy and labored hard for the cause.

Robert E. Lee, up to then a career officer in the Union service, abhorred the idea of disunion. Wrote Lee, "I can contemplate no greater calamity for the country than a dissolution of the Union. Still a Union that can only be maintained by swords and bayonets, and in which strife and civil war are to take the place of brotherly love and kindness, has no love for me."

The war created enormous financial problems in both the North and the South. Both sides resorted to paper money extensively to finance the war. Gold and silver (specie) of Virginia banks went into Confederate securities that ultimately became worthless.

It seems almost unthinkable that the nation's growth would be brought down by a cruel and wasteful debacle of the magnitude of the Civil War.

The Old Dominion, with population of 1,219,630 in 1860, had been the leading Southern state, and prior to the war most of the market centers such as Norfolk, Richmond and Petersburg, were prospering on agricultural trade.

Governor John Letcher, required by law to report to the Senate and House of Delegates, reported on banking as of January 26, 1861. On September 30, 1860, the capital of all the banks in Virginia was $16,566,510, and their circulation was $9,806,837.

Their circulation, therefore, fell short of their capital, $6,759,672.17, Letcher observed.

He chastised some of the bankers for failing to keep their circulation sufficiently high for revenue purposes. The banks were taxed at the rate of 17 percent on their note circulation. Other banks came in for praise for responding to the revenue need.

Letcher told the legislators that "the revenue of the state is derived from the circulation of the various banks within her limits. Is not circulation, then, the fair basis of calculation for the contribution of specie that the state may require to meet her wants?"

Some bankers had held a meeting in Richmond to object to the method of calculating the tax requisition from their banks.

The report by Governor Letcher revealed that Virginia borrowed $50,000 from the Farmers Bank of Virginia, and "a like sum" from the Bank of Virginia on June 30, 1860. The large sum was required to pay the interest on the state debt of the first of January, and to redeem "the portion of the debt that had then to be taken in" shows it was indispensable to raise it in funds equivalent to coin; and there was no mode of raising it, except by distributing the amount among all the banks in the state, he declared.

In conclusion, Letcher said, "I recommend that you adopt the necessary legislation to require the banks to furnish the requisite amount of coin or specie funds to meet the demands for interest and redemption that will fall due on the first day of July next, and on the first day of July 1862, and subsequently, until there shall be a resumption of specie payments. I recommend also that the act shall prescribe the rule for the contribution by the banks."

Letcher's report, compiled by the Treasury Office in Richmond, January 26, 1861, listed 25 chartered banks in Virginia (which at that time included what is now West Virginia). The compilation showed the amount that each bank would pay at the circulating rate of 17 percent. Only two had paid, the Bank of Old Dominion and the Fairmont Bank.

Following is the tabular statement from reports of the banks in Virginia, January 1, 1862, reported from the Executive Department as of February 8, 1862. Note that 22 state banks are listed. No reports were received from the Bank of the Valley, Bank of Howardsville, Bank of Philippi, Bank of the Old Dominion, Fairmont Bank, Northwestern Bank of Virginia (except from the Jeffersonville branch), and Merchants and Mechanics Bank of Wheeling.

The report commented: "The circulation of the above banks has been largely increased in proportion to the specie, by loans to the Confederate States and to the state of Virginia."

The reports did not include the private, unchartered banks that performed as banks of the time. One such institution, Burke & Herbert, founded in 1852 in Alexandria, continued to operate during the war. It continues today as Virginia's

TABULAR STATEMENT,

Made up from the reports of the banks of this commonwealth, of January 1st, 1862, as required by act of assembly.

NAMES OF BANKS.	Capital.	Circulation.	Specie.	Deposits.	Discounts.
Merchants Bank of Virginia, Lynchburg, - - - - -	417900 00	328412.00	95497 00	114864 33	345805 97
Bank of the Commonwealth, - - - - -	1074300 00	358441 00	61981 23	972177 44	778035 99
Southwestern Bank of Virginia, Wytheville, - - -	161300 00	179083 00	36611 94	159232 79	130995 28
Bank of Rockbridge, - - - - -	125000 00	126065 00	10466 00	95507 91	112763 08
Danville Bank, - - - - -	300000 00	234078 00	47712 28	70332 03	499042 24
Northwestern Bank of Virginia (Jeffersonville branch), - -	164200 00	205970 00	52174 20	24375 59	315953 55
Bank of Pittsylvania, - - - - -	150310 00	147864 00	35165 76	4155 44	197755 96
Farmers Bank of Fincastle, - - - - -	160000 00	164265 00	15453 73	50298 91	112801 12
Traders Bank of the City of Richmond, - - - - -	306110 00	122290 00	30912 61	586773 56	407826 94
Bank of Virginia, - - - - -	2651250 00	1390438 83	449290 10	3855696 06	3422365 78
Bank of Richmond, - - - - -	130195 00	64500 00	9624 15	133628 58	125648 83
Bank of Commerce, Fredericksburg, - - - - -	158100 00	135930 00	24980 89	161352 08	154771 93
Bank of Berkeley, - - - - -	10000 00	48680 00	15860 46	36409 61	49104 16
Bank of Winchester, - - - - -	113000 00	100887 00	16030 69	212933 53	142075 48
Bank of Scottsville, - - - - -	100000 00	145424 00	29254 78	17418 69	195417 78
Bank of Charleston (now at Richmond), - - - - -	300000 00	84542 50	23548 05	18819 51	183847 63
Bank of the City of Petersburg - - - - -	300000 00	151000 00	32088 21	378709 91	530011 63
Central Bank of Virginia, Staunton, - - - - -	201400 00	307911 00	45732 77	273178 50	264179 47
Monticello Bank, Charlottesville, - - - - -	333300 00	442973 00	45240 50	160641 70	465409 52
Farmers Bank of Virginia, - - - - -	3150900 00	1901103 00	416120 40	4959758 77	4856915 00
Bank of Rockingham, - - - - -	213200 00	222679 00	22998 23	243297 42	149500 63
Exchange Bank of Virginia, - - - - -	2721300 00	1558308 50	352111 91	3281856 07	3439966 13
	$13331765 00	8420851 83	1859856 00	15812420 34	16789295 99

oldest bank. Some of its experiences during the occupation of Alexandria are recalled in the following chapter.

Bankers were not overlooked by the Confederate Congress, of course. A tax of 50 cents per share at par value of $100 was collected by the banks. Hungry for revenue, the Confederacy also taxed cash on hand as well as money on loan at interest.

The Provisional Congress of the Confederate States of America authorized a $15 million loan on February 28, 1861, to yield eight percent interest. A windfall for the Confederate treasury was the result of the capture of the U.S. Mint and custom house in New Orleans. The capture got $389,267.46 from the mint and $147,519.66 from customs, held by Louisiana and transferred to the Confederate treasury, a gift "that the Congress of the Confederate States of America accepts with a high sense of the partriotic liberality of the State of Louisiana the funds so generously donated to the treasury of the Confederate States." A draft of the United States for $300,000 was returned dishonored.

The Confederacy immediately authorized treasury notes of $1 million to bear interest at one cent per day per hundred.

The Confederates immediately authorized treasury notes of $1 million to bear interest at one cent per day per hundred.

As the war drained the limited resources, note issues bore interest at two cents per day per hundred dollars or 7.30 percent.

Secretary of the Treasury Christopher Memminger gave the war cost at $215 million per month. At that rate, the Confederate treasury would be bankrupt at the beginning of 1864, Robert Tombs of Georgia predicted.

Men were at war instead of growing food and fiber. Mrs. Jefferson Davis in Richmond listed the costs of commodity prices in February 1863: Bacon, $6 lb.; ham, $7 lb.; turkeys, $60 each; firewood, $35 per cord; board for a horse at the Richmond livery stable, $300 per month; flour, $300 per barrel; fish, $5 per lb.; and the prices continued to rise until 1865 when a suit of clothes cost $2,700, six yards of linen, $1,200. The cost of a shave and haircut was $10. The price for an ounce of quinine was $1,700, and was $50 for a cake of soap.

All reality of orderly financing of the war disappeared. President Davis wrote that little or no records were kept of the amount of notes issued after July 1864. An estimated $1.2 billion in notes were in circulation. Total currency in circulation—Confederate, state banks, corporations, merchants and railroads—was $2.2 billion at the close of the war. This has been figured to be about $225 per capita.

As the closing days of the war approached, the Confederate Congress passed a joint resolution soliciting contributions to the treasury. People responded, sending in various items such as bonds, currency, coin, family heirlooms, keepsakes, jewelry and silverware. Although the state taxes were high, the Confederate taxes were a problem, particularly an occupation tax that ranged from $50 to $200 and the gross sales of business of merchants, brokers, lawyers, auctioneers, bankers, butchers, druggists—and others. Hotels paid from $30 to $500. Commodity trading was taxed at 10 percent. A charge of 8 percent was paid for agricultural products on hand. One tax that aggravated the people was the "tax in kind" that required producers of agricultural products to turn over to the government 10 percent of their production, above a certain base exemption, and the farmer had to deliver the products to the nearest railroad station.

Peace negotiations fell apart in early February 1865 when President Abraham Lincoln and Secretary of State William H. Seward met Confederate Vice President Alexander Stephens, Robert M.T. Hunter and J.A. Campbell aboard the *River Queen,* a Union transport, in Hampton Roads. President Jefferson Davis had instructed his negotiators to insist upon Southern independence.

At Five Forks, April 1, 1865, the decisive battle between Lee and Grant took place. Union casualties totaled 802; Confederate, 4,444.

President Davis and other officials gathered up important papers, some gold, and left Richmond. Other retreating Confederates torched warehouses. The flames, out of control, engulfed other buildings, destroying most of the business district, including banking buildings. Altogether, over 900 buildings were destroyed. Richmond was surrendered to Union soldiers on April 3, and they were ordered to help put out the raging inferno. Military government was instituted in the city. "So great was the destitution in Richmond that the Federal authorities had to issue rations to keep the impoverished from starving," a local historian wrote.

With no banks, all Confederate bonds and money worthless and most of the gold of the banks having been shipped south, the end of the Confederacy had come.

Word came of General Lee's surrender at Appomattox on April 9. Frances Leigh Williams, writing in *A Century of Service,* a history of First and Merchants National Bank, Richmond, said, "It was a situation that called for courage based on a totally realistic appraisal of the situation as it existed. It was a time when the needs of men were more important than preference, pride, or despair over what was lost."

General Lee told his officers, "The wise thing to do is to accommodate ourselves to the new order of things, go home, and go to work."

Virginia was impoverished. The people had little left but "their battle swept fields." Virginians worked to produce a prosperous Old Dominion but kept fast the strong tradition for principle and character, individual freedom, and held on to its best traditions.

2

Hiding Specie and Saving Mount Vernon Funds

The bank's silver was buried in a sarcophagus in Charlottesville. —Story of the cashier of the Bank of the Old Dominion, Alexandria, who saved the bank's gold and silver.

WHEN FEDERAL TROOPS MARCHED across the Potomac to Alexandria in May 1861, plans were set in motion to save local assets from confiscation by the invaders.

Through the action by a discount clerk at the Bank of Old Dominion, the financial integrity of the bank was enhanced.

As the occupation troops approached the old city, J.W. Lockwood decided to transfer the gold out of the town and store it in safer vaults, such as those in Lynchburg and Richmond. By moving the assets around, he avoided their cap-

National Bank of Fredericksburg, formerly a branch of the Farmers Bank, founded in 1812, closed by the Civil War, has been restored and includes a first-rate museum.
(Courtesy First National Bank)

ture. Upon the evacuation of Richmond, $2,000 in silver was buried in a sarcophagus in Charlottesville. When hostilities ended, Lockwood dug up the valuable silver, recovered the gold that he had protected, and two months later "returned it to the board of directors."

The Farmers Bank of Federicksburg was founded in 1812. During the Civil War the city changed hands seven times before the hostilities ended, according to Lemuel W. Houston, author of *The First National Bank of Fredericksburg.*

By the end of the war the old city was in ruins, destroyed by the battles. Dr. John Hooe Wallace had given up his medical practice in 1860 to devote full time to managing the bank. At the beginning of the war most of the bank's employees joined the Confederate Army, leaving Dr. Wallace and the cashier behind. "Early in the war it was deemed prudent for the cashier to remove the bank's funds and records to Danville for safe-keeping," Houston wrote. Dr. Wallace, who had been president of the bank for 25 years, held on as long as he could. "Finally, however, he was forced to abandon the handsome brick building when it was taken over as headquarters of Federal troops then occupying Fredericksburg," the author said.

It never reopened as the Farmers Bank. The building was sold in October 1865 to the newly chartered National Bank of Fredericksburg. It has since been fully restored and houses a first-rate museum, a service to the community and banking history.

Many other stories are told about the actions taken to preserve the integrity of bank funds.

Certainly one of the most unusual stories of loyalty and evasive action involved the Burke & Herbert Bank in Alexandria.

Bonds and money were paid by the Mount Vernon Ladies Association in order to acquire Mount Vernon from its last private owner, John Augustine Washington, Jr. The bank's history tells the story.

Most of the funds amounting to $200,000 were deposited in the Burke & Herbert Bank, guarded by both the Burke and Herbert families "to the extent of placing their lives in jeopardy."

The Union troops found out about the Mount Vernon funds in the bank and demanded that they be surrendered, but they were told that the Washington deposit was no longer there.

"Anticipating just such an attempt at confiscation, Mr. Burke had taken his friend's treasure home with him and placed it under some clothing in his wife's closet," the history reports. The Union troops and their leader showed up at the Burke residence for a search. Mrs. Burke kept the secret. The searchers went to Mrs. Burke's room and opened the closet door.

When asked about the closet, she replied: "Why, that is my closet, as you see. It has my clothes in it. Don't you want to search it?"

"No, madam," one of the troops replied. "It is not my wish to search a lady's closet."

"No, Madam," one of the troops replied. "It is not my wish to search a lady's closet."

Miss Sarah C. Tracy had come to Mount Vernon from Troy, New York. The Herberts and Burkes were good friends of Miss Tracy, who, as a Northerner, passed through the lines from Mount Vernon to Alexandria at will. According to the published story, Miss Tracy came to town in a wagon with a basket of fresh eggs for sale at the market. The book *Presence of a Lady,* by Dorothy T. Muir, states that Miss Tracy stopped by the Burke residence on the way to the market. Mr. Burke asked, "Would you be willing to do a great favor for the Washington family?"

"I will do anything for them that is within my power," she is quoted as replying.

The package was brought, eggs removed, and the valuables placed in the bottom of the basket covered by the fresh eggs. "Take the package to Mr. Riggs at the bank in Washington and say it comes from a friend across the river," Burke told the young woman. She took the basket, got on the wagon, and rode down the streets of Alexandria, past some 75,000 Union soldiers. Armed with her Federal pass, she crossed over the bridge, and entered the city of Washington. She drove directly to Mr. Riggs' office, in the bank, rented a safe deposit box, placed the package of money and bonds inside, and locked the box. Then with a brief explanation and farewell to Mr. Riggs, she drove back across the Potomac and gave the key to the box to Mr. Burke. To avoid suspicion, she had left her eggs on Mr. Riggs desk, where she emptied them from her basket, and with her usual thoughtfulness, she had tucked the egg money in her little purse.

John Augustine Washington held a commission as a colonel under General Lee as one of his aides. He lost his life on September 13, 1861, and Mrs. Washington died soon thereafter.

The story of Virginia's oldest bank was written by Dorothy Holcombe Kabler and published by the bank on the occasion of its 100th anniversary in 1952.

3

A New System—National Banks

He had said that no duty on the federal government was more imperative "than the duty it owes its people of furnishing them a sound and uniform currency."
—Bray Hammond, banking historian, referring to Abraham Lincoln

WHEN ABRAHAM LINCOLN TOOK OFFICE on March 4, 1861, he inherited a nation that was in a severe financial plight. Members of Congress had not been paid for several weeks, and the embarrassing debacle was blamed on low tariff revenues. Congress turned to temporary measures for relief, such as issuing bonds and floating bank loans.

Lincoln named Samuel Portland Chase, a competent lawyer from Ohio, as

A cartouche that banks used in ordering their bank notes printed prior to the national banking system.
(Courtesy of the Author)

Secretary of the Treasury. He had been Governor of Ohio, but had only modest experience in finance. He was a "hard money" specie man who frowned on bank paper as a remedy for financial problems.

While a member of the Illinois legislature, Lincoln was a strong advocate of a national bank. On the other hand, Chase disliked and generally distrusted banks, and he opposed a central bank. His favorite currency, he said in 1856, would be a "currency of coin." What Chase found when he came to the cabinet was "enough to stagger a financial genius." The government had not levied internal taxes of any sort for forty years. There was no system for efficient administration. The Independent Treasury System required all federal transactions to be in coin or Treasury notes. Faced with these realities, Chase resorted to issuing bonds to finance war-related expenses.

By December 1862, Chase renewed his support for national bank-note currency, backed by United States securities. He added something new—the suggestion that this currency should be issued by "banking associations organized under national legislation—with national instead of state charters." The state banks would be urged to switch to national charters. President Lincoln followed these discussions intently; he became a staunch supporter of the national bank note-currency proposal. Strong opposition came from various quarters, both in and out of Congress, but Lincoln lobbied hard for the legislation as a war finance measure.

In a moment of deep concern, he asked in January 1862, "What shall I do? The people are impatient; Chase has no more money and he tells me he can raise no more .... The bottom is out of the tub." Thirteen months later, however, Congress passed the National Bank Act and Lincoln signed it into law on February 25, 1863.

The law permitted nationally chartered banks to issue national bank notes up to 90 percent of the amount of Government bonds they held. Uniform in design, each bank was required to redeem its notes, and for the first time the counterfeiting of national bank notes became a Federal crime.

The notes had the confidence of the people. Congress in 1865 put a 10 percent Federal tax on all state bank notes. Hugh McCulloch, president of the State Bank of Indiana, was a vocal and able opponent of the national banks. A near miracle happened when McCulloch accepted Lincoln's appointment as the first Comptroller of the Currency. He set forth to establish the office as a major force in the nation's financial history. His office began on a modest operation—with five clerks and a messenger—within the Treasury.

A story was told about Lincoln, that at a cabinet meeting a suggestion was made that the greenbacks bear the words, "In God We Trust" as did the silver coins. Lincoln thought a moment and suggested that if any legend was to be put

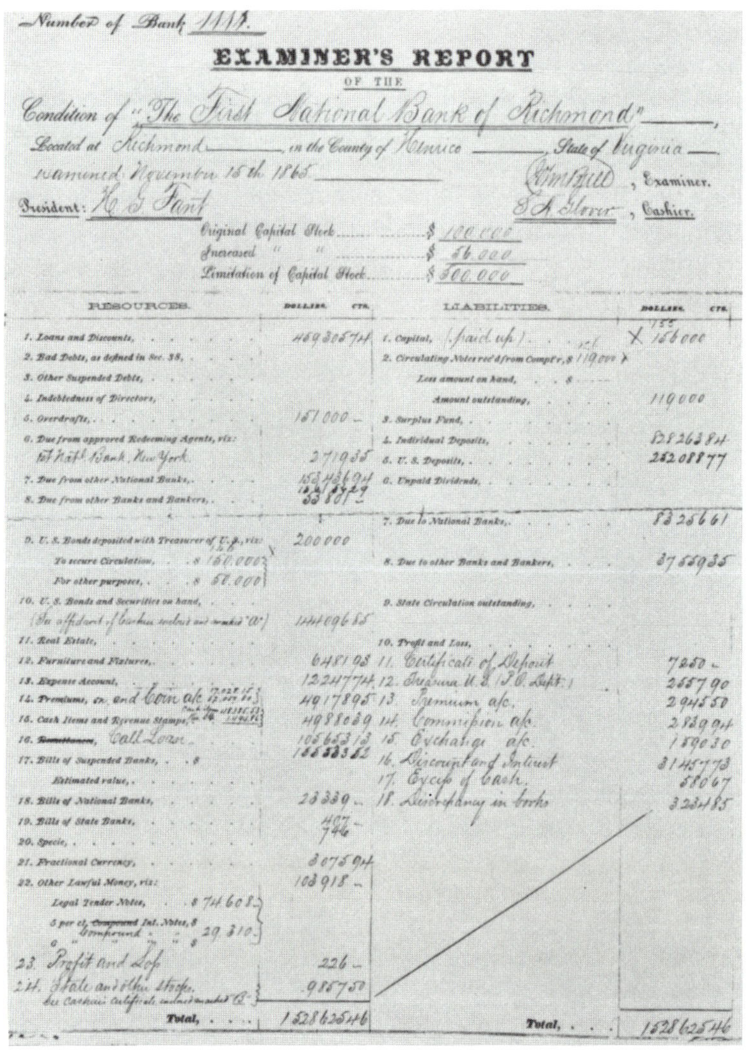

Number of Bank 1111.

EXAMINER'S REPORT

OF THE

Condition of "The First National Bank of Richmond",
Located at Richmond, in the County of Henrico, State of Virginia
Examined November 15th 1865
Examiner.
President: H. G. Fant
S. A. Glover, Cashier.

Original Capital Stock $ 100 000
Increased " " $ 56 000
Limitation of Capital Stock $ 500 000

RESOURCES.	DOLLARS. CTS.
1. Loans and Discounts,	469305 74
2. Bad Debts, as defined in Sec. 38,	
3. Other Suspended Debts,	
4. Indebtedness of Directors,	
5. Overdrafts,	151 000 –
6. Due from approved Redeeming Agents, viz: 1st Natl Bank, New York.	2719 35
7. Due from other National Banks,	152486 94
8. Due from other Banks and Bankers,	33 801 –
9. U. S. Bonds deposited with Treasurer of U. S., viz: To secure Circulation, $ 150 000; For other purposes, $ 50 000	200 000
10. U. S. Bonds and Securities on hand, (See affidavit of Cashier enclosed and marked "A")	144 096 55
11. Real Estate,	
12. Furniture and Fixtures,	6481 98
13. Expense Account,	12247 74
14. Premiums, &c. and Coin a/c	49178 95
15. Cash Items and Revenue Stamps,	49880 39
16. ~~Remittances~~, Call Loan	105653 13
17. Bills of Suspended Banks, $ Estimated value,	
18. Bills of National Banks,	23339 –
19. Bills of State Banks,	407 –
20. Specie,	746
21. Fractional Currency,	3075 94
22. Other Lawful Money, viz: Legal Tender Notes, $ 74 608; 5 per ct. ~~Compound~~ Int. Notes, Compound $ 29 310	103 918 –
23. Profit and Loss	226 –
24. State and other Stocks. See Cashier's Certificate enclosed marked "B"	9857 50
Total,	1528625 46

LIABILITIES.	DOLLARS. CTS.
1. Capital, (paid up)	156 000
2. Circulating Notes rec'd from Compt'r, $ 119 000; Less amount on hand, $; Amount outstanding,	119 000
3. Surplus Fund,	
4. Individual Deposits,	528263 84
5. U. S. Deposits,	252088 77
6. Unpaid Dividends,	
7. Due to National Banks,	83 256 61
8. Due to other Banks and Bankers,	37 559 35
9. State Circulation outstanding,	
10. Profit and Loss,	
11. Certificate of Deposit	7250 –
12. Treasurer U. S. (P. O. Dept.)	2557 90
13. Premium a/c.	2945 50
14. Commission a/c.	2839 94
15. Exchange a/c.	1590 30
16. Discount and Interest	31457 73
17. Excess of Cash.	580 67
18. Discrepancy in books	3234 85
Total,	1528625 46

Photo of the first bank examiner's report on November 15, 1865, of the First National Bank of Richmond.
(From A Century of Service, First & Merchants National Bank, 1965)

on the bills, it should be that of Peter and John: "Silver and gold have I none, but such as I have I give thee."

The system of national banks and state chartered banks become the dual banking system, a system that continues.

Virginia became active within a week after Lee's surrender. A small number of men in Richmond decided to cooperate with some "well-established northerners" to do something about the desperate need for banking. They met on April 17, 1865, in Richmond to hammer out a plan to establish the city's first national bank under the National Banking Act. They agreed that a national charter would be sought and that the bank would be called The First National Bank of Virginia. The bank opened for business on May 10, 1865.

Only a few days after the First National Bank was organized, The National Bank of Virginia and the Exchange National Bank were chartered. Planters National Bank was among the earliest of the national banks, chartered on December 8, 1865. Also among the earliest chartered were: the Merchants National Bank of Richmond; the Peoples National Bank of Lynchburg; the Lynchburg National Bank; the Norfolk National Bank; and the City National Bank of Norfolk.

The first state banks chartered after the Civil War were savings banks: The Planters Savings Bank, Richmond; Planters Savings Bank, Farmville; Rockbridge Savings Bank, Lexington; Farmers and Mechanics Bank, Covington; Botetourt Savings Bank, Buchanan; and the Virginia Savings Bank, Richmond—all established within the same month. In March 1866, the Commercial Savings Bank, Richmond; the Christiansburg Savings Institution; and the Union Bank of Richmond, were incorporated.

From the outset, the national banks were required to make reports to the Comptroller of the Currency. No records were kept of state banks until the year 1885, when a law became effective that required all banks to make reports to the Auditor of Public Accounts.

At first it was feared that the national banks would virtually eliminate state banks, but that did not happen.

The system of national banks and state chartered banks resulted in the dual banking system, a system that continues.

4

Inching Forward on the Road to a New Day

"Nothing succeeds like success."
—English proverb

THORNY QUESTIONS, tensions in a time of transition, and complicated political issues faced Virginia and the nation.

"We hoped," wrote Ralph Waldo Emerson, "that in the peace ... a great expansion would follow in the mind of the country; grand views in every direction .... But the energy of the nation seemed to have expended itself." He meant moral energy, of course.

During the hostilities the loss of life was heavy. Most of the railways had been destroyed; roads had been neglected; livestock was in short supply; armies on the march had destroyed much of the agriculture; fences, homes, outbuildings had been burned or were in ruins.

"The country between Washington and Richmond was ... like a desert," one contemporary report said.

Cities, as we have seen, fared poorly. Industry had been destroyed or abandoned; financial institutions were bankrupt; credit resources for business were gone; the Reconstruction government took over. Virginia was not readmitted to the Union until January 26, 1870. For the first time in five years Virginia members of Congress were permitted to occupy their legislative seats.

Virginians began rebuilding the nearly prostrate economic base, something they had to do on their own. The struggle to make a living began.

Virginia's population in 1880 was 1,512,565. On May 31 that year there were a total of 76 banks. Of these, 20 were private banks without charter, and two were savings banks. The combined capital was $3,036,974, and deposits totaled $7,757,202. According to John Jay Knox, there were the same number in 1890, but the deposits had grown to $13,767,424. And on June 30, 1899, there were 89 banks with deposits of $21,106,121. The report for 1889 showed Virginia had 35 national banks and deposits of $16,402,000.

Richmond's clearing house reports showed clearing for August 1899 at $13,074,218.

Concludes Knox, "Banking in Virginia had prospered generally and shows a steady growth." Both state and national banks participated in this growth. On September 7, 1899, the national banks in the Old Dominion numbered 36. There were 72 state banks of discount and deposit, 11 savings banks, and six trust companies.

One of the conditions holding back the number of national banks chartered was the $50,000 capital required at the beginning; later the amount was reduced to $25,000.

One of the first of the state banks organized after the Civil War was the Citizens Bank of Norfolk, chartered by the Virginia legislature in 1867. It had $300,000 capital. Another was the Bank of Portsmouth. The Bank of the State of Virginia was chartered by the circuit court of Richmond on January 10, 1870, having a capital of $500,000, at that time the largest state bank.

The Old Dominion's economy moved slowly upward; so did its banks.

PART FOUR

Virginia Bankers Association —Why?

1

The Meeting in Richmond in 1893

"The convention of Virginia Bankers, the movement for which was inaugurated by Mr. H.M. Darnall, of Roanoke, was called to order in the restaurant room of the Chamber of Commerce at noon ...."
—News account of the meeting in Richmond held on Wednesday, October 11, 1893

CONCERNED BANKERS MET IN RICHMOND at a time of national crisis, the severe Panic of 1893. The stock market had dropped in May to a record low. Anxiety filled the air as banks called in their loans.

Richmond bankers were able to handle the "currency famine" until late summer. Then, they were forced to protect their banks when customers in such cities as New York, Baltimore and Washington found themselves unable to put up currency against their outstanding balances. The Richmond Clearing House decided not to pay out currency amounting to $50 or less.

An entirely different event had happened in 1893 on a northbound night express operated by the Richmond, Fredericksburg, and Potomac Railroad. Masked men boarded the train at Aquia Creek and made off with $50,000 from the express car. This was listed as the first train robbery in Virginia. The robbers later were arrested and they confessed to the crime.

The year 1893 was reviewed on January 1, 1894, in the *Dispatch* in the follow-

Henry M. Darnall, Roanoke banker, promoted the organization of the Virginia Bankers Association.

ing manner: "Richmond's banking and general financial record for 1893 affords a striking demonstration of her solidity, the confidence of the people in the management of these institutions, and of the fact that the current of business, while it naturally lost in volume, kept flowing in conservative channels ...."

In a remarkable show of cooperation, the press reported that "All departments of trade stood shoulder to shoulder with the banks in the matter [use of certified check system except for small checks for a period of weeks], and the banks in turn did everything in their power to carry their customrs. The result was that the banks came out of the flurry unscathed, and there were few business failures of any moment."

Henry Mauze Darnall, a prominent Roanoke business and civic leader, was one of the primary forces behind the formation of the Virginia Bankers Association. He had long felt the need for bankers to organize. This insistence paid off, and the Virginia Bankers Association became a reality on Thursday, October 11, 1893.

The following is from the Richmond *Dispatch* of that day:

> THE BANKERS CONVENTION TO-DAY/Conference Last Night with Reference to a Constitution and By-Laws/Mr. H.M. Darnall of Roanoke, who started the movement for a convention of the Virginia bankers here to organize a State bankers' association, arrived in the city yesterday morning, and last night held a conference at the Westmoreland Club, with Major W.J. Johnson, Mr. John N. Ellett, Mr. John P. Branch, and Colonel W.H. Palmer, the committee of the clearing-house appointed to meet him, and prepare business for the convention. The conference considered a constitution and by-laws for the association, the offices of which it is proposed, shall consist of a president, nine vice-presidents, a secretary, and a treasurer. It is also proposed that there be an executive committee of seven or nine members, a committee on finance, and a committee on banking and jurisprudence.
>
> The convention will meet at noon today in the restaurant of the Chamber of Commerce, and will probably hold their sessions during the day. It is expected that there will be about one hundred delegates present. At

The Westmoreland Club in Richmond where the VBA delegates met on October 11, 1893.

> night the visitors will be entertained at the Westmoreland Club.
>
> Governor McKinney yesterday received an invitation from Major Johnson to attend both the convention and the entertainment.
>
> Colonel Walter H. Taylor, of Norfolk, and Mr. C.M. Blackford, of Lynchburg, are spoken of for president of the association.

The delegates—bankers and heroes—were ready for significant action.

The delegates—bankers and heroes—were ready for significant action. In the middle of the depression, the group felt that the formation of an association for bankers to combine the interests of banks for harmonious action would give still greater assurance that all other interests dependent upon banking were in safe hands and the deposits of the people were safe. "The bankers of Virginia had thoroughly demonstrated that they wanted the confidence of the people," a report said.

The Westmoreland Club was a men's club, which occupied the elegant former home of William H. Macfarland, early Richmond banker, at 6th and Grace Streets.

Twenty-eight years had passed since the war had ended, but many of the business, civic and political leaders had served in the Confederacy. As they gathered at the Westmoreland Club and glanced at the gallery of portraits of distinguished Southern soldiers and statesmen, they felt at home.

One of the meetings which followed the formation of the Virginia Bankers Association was held in Richmond on September 18, 1894. The opening address was made by Aubind L. Boulware, president of First National, and the local press carried a story about the gathering. According to the story, "Mr. Boulware told the bankers that the panic of 1893 may well have been a blessing in disguise as the favorable way the emergency had been handled in the South had created new national interest in the abilities of Southern businessmen."

2

Walter Herron Taylor, the Colonel From Norfolk

"Few men have been more honored in life than was Colonel Walter H. Taylor ...."
—Richmond Times-Dispatch

THE DELEGATES TO THE FIRST MEETING of the Virginia Bankers Association in Richmond on October 11, 1893, selected Walter Herron Taylor to be the first president.

Why was the 55-year-old bank president from Norfolk the overwhelming choice?

Born in Norfolk June 13, 1838, he excelled in school, including the Virginia Military Institute. After three years at VMI he left at the death of his father during the yellow fever epidemic of 1855. After returning to Norfolk, his first business experience was at the Norfolk branch of the Bank of Virginia and even at an early age he was recognized as a "highly successful banker" with astute business sense. Before the outbreak of the Civil War he also had attained the rank of lieutenant in a Norfolk militia company. With the outbreak of hostilities, Taylor was recommended to General Robert E. Lee. Virginia Governor John Letcher, at Lee's recommendation, ordered the "serious-minded young officer from Norfolk to Richmond and assigned him to Lee's headquarters with the rank of captain."

Taylor was with Lee at every battle, but would not attend the surrender signing at Appomattox, April 9, 1865, because he "could not endure the thought of seeing that heroic soul bowed in agony by the last blow of fate."

With the breakup of the Confederate army, "all officers bade farewell to Lee except Taylor, who rode with him back to Richmond and posed on the back porch of the Lee home on Franklin Street for the famous Brady photograph with Lee and his son Custis."

Colonel Taylor married after the war and returned to his hometown of Norfolk to live. He became president of the Marine Bank and held the office until his death March 1, 1916, at age 77. By order of the legislature, flags on all state buildings flew at half-mast.

After the war, Taylor authored *Four Years with General Lee,* a classic book that was published in 1877. Historians, including Douglas Southall Freeman, have noted that Taylor had a clear memory of his Civil War experiences long after the conflict ended.

Thus, it is not surprising that the bankers who gathered in Richmond in 1893 were well aware of Taylor's accomplishments, including the fact that he was the youngest member of Lee's staff.

As one writer commented, "To have lived so that all men gave him reverence

The Virginia Bankers Association knew that its gavel was in the best of hands.

to the day of his death is memory fine enough, but to have lived so that in his youth he was a trusted adjutant of Robert E. Lee sets his name apart and emblazons it."

The Virginia Bankers Association knew that its gavel was in the best of hands.

Many tributes to Colonel Taylor have been written and said over the years. George H. Tucker, writing in the *Virginian-Pilot,* June 26, 1972, brought out many interesting facts about his life and career, and a part of the article follows:

"Colonel Walter Herron Taylor, Norfolk's most influential post-Civil War citizen and aide de camp of Gen. Robert E. Lee from 1861-1865, grew so accus-

Photograph above was made by Brady on the back porch of General Lee's residence on Franklin Street in Richmond. Colonel Taylor, at right, accompanied Lee from Appomattox to Richmond. At left, is Custis, General Lee's son.
(From Four Years With General Lee, by Colonel Taylor)

1. H.S. TROUT, Prest. First National Bank, Roanoke.
2. COL. WALTER H. TAYLOR, Prest. Marine Bank, Norfolk.
3. R. W. BURKE, Prest. Nat'l Valley Bank, Staunton.
4. WM. M. HILL, Cashier State Bank of Va., Richmond.
5. MANN S. QUARLES, V.P. Va. Trust Co., Richmond.
6. CALDWELL HARDY, Prest. Norfolk Nat'l. Bank, Norfolk.
7. OLIVER J. SANDS, Prest. Amer. Nat'l Bank, Richmond.
8. C. D. FISHBURNE, Cash. Bk. of Albe'm'le, Charlottesville.
9. GEO. J. SEAY, of Scott & Stringfellow, Richmond.
10. HENRY L. SCHMELZ, Prest. Bank of Hampton, Hampton

(From VBA Proceedings, 1904)

tomed to obeying orders from his illustrious commander during the war that he continued to take orders from him even after peace was proclaimed.

"Colonel Taylor married Miss Elizabeth Selder Saunders in Richmond on April 3, 1865, and returned to Norfolk with his bride shortly after Appomattox.

"Their first four children were girls, and Colonel Taylor promptly announced their births to his old commander as they appeared on the scene.

"Finally, after the arrival of the last daughter, Gen. Lee suggested it was high time to match the four girls with an equal number of boys, an order Col. Taylor dutifully obeyed.

"After the balance had been restored by the arrival of the fourth son, Mrs. Taylor remarked laconically: 'Walter became so used to signing "By Order of General Lee. Walter H. Taylor, A.A.G." during the war, he even followed the rule when it came to having a family.'"

The first VBA convention was held in November 1894 in Norfolk. Another Confederate veteran was elected president, Henry S. Trout of Roanoke, who was a prosperous farmer and was called from the farm to later become president of the First National Bank of Roanoke, when it was organized in 1882.

Trout, born on October 15, 1841, served as lieutenant, Company I, Twenty-Eighth Virginia Infantry, Pickett's Division. At war's end he was released from Johnson's Island, where he was a prisoner of war.

Trout was involved with the development of Roanoke and assisted in the laying out of the city. In 1892 he became mayor of Roanoke. He was a member of the House of Delegates from 1877 to 1881 and in the Senate from 1882 to 1886.

The third VBA president was Caldwell Hardy of Norfolk (1896-97). When the Norfolk National Bank was organized in 1885, he became cashier, and was named president in 1899. He was also president of the Norfolk Bank for Savings and Trusts.

Hardy was active in the American Bankers Association. He was a member of the executive council for two years, was elected ABA first vice president in 1901, and advanced to the ABA presidency in 1902, the first ABA head from Virginia. He served as an officer of the Federal Reserve Bank of Richmond to round out his career.

Banking associations were slow in getting started. Not until 1875 was the American Bankers Association organized at Saratoga Springs, New York. Bankers around the nation, including Virginia, were stimulated by the ABA's success. The Texas Bankers Association became the first state banking association, organized in 1885.

Evidence continued to mount that state bankers associations were of growing significance. Bankers were living in the real world.

The discerning Frenchman Alexis de Tocqueville, on his visit to the United States in 1830, noted that "Americans of all ages, all stations in life ... are forever forming associations." He strongly supported the value of associations to a free society through voluntary coooperative action.

Said he, "In countries where such associations do not exist, if private people do not ... create something like them, I see no other dike to hold back tyranny of whatever sort, and a great nation might with impunity be oppressed by some tiny faction or by a single man."

National expansion advanced the notion of associations. Early on, the VBA became the appropriate organization to bring bankers—private and chartered—together for a common mission.

The VBA's first constitution noted its objectives: "In order to promote the general welfare and usefulness of banks and banking institutions; to cultivate more intimate, social and business relations between members; to collect and disseminate valuable financial and economic information affecting our common interests; to secure unity and cooperation in the furtherance of legitimate and conservative banking, and for the purpose of correct information as to the functions of banks, and their relation to the commercial, industrial and agricultural interests of the State, we submit the following Constitution for the Virginia Bankers Association."

3

Virginia Recognition—The 1900 ABA Convention Meets in Richmond

"Trigg, I am going right straight to New York and advise the Council to have its Convention in Richmond."
—Walker Hill, St. Louis banker and president of the ABA

THE TWENTY-SIXTH ANNUAL CONVENTION of the American Bankers AssocViaiton met in Richmond, October 2-4, 1900. Bankers from every state attended. The Jefferson was the convention hotel.

Gracious welcomes were extended by Virginia Governor J. Hodge Tyler. He used humor and elegant rhetoric to say: "The bank and the bankers form thc common meeting place for the energies and enterprises of the people. They constitute a common reservoir, into which empty the thousands of streams of human thrift and ingenuity and out of which are drawn irrigating and sustaining currents of capital for carrying on exchanges and trades among men and for developing the latent powers of nature. The banker is the most trusted of all men, and, in turn, he must, perforce, maintain the greatest faith in others."

J.P. Lewis, Martinsville, said, "I am here to say that Virginia is probably the equal of any state in the Union. What she needs is progressive men and some money to develop her resources."

William R. Trigg, Richmond, reported on the condition of banks in the state for the VBA president, Mann S. Quarles. To use his own words, "From every standpoint the outlook is encouraging to us, both as bankers and as Virginians."

Virginius Newton, president of the Richmond Clearing-House Association, extended the welcome of his group. Said he, "One old enough to have borne his part in the momentous days of our Civil War—when the new birth of the Nation passed through convulsive throes, more crucial than in any epoch of its checkered life—yet young enough to recall, with vividness, the heroic and strenuous play of vital forces, now happily tempered by the silent, ceaseless torch of Time, may but regard this day as one of the most conspicuous in the calends of the capital of the late Confederacy." One of the most significant actions to be approved by the Richmond convention was the creation of the Institute of Bank Clerks, which became the American Institute of Banking.

At the time of the convention, Caldwell Hardy, Norfolk banker, was chairman of the ABA Executive Council. He became ABA president in 1902.

Col. J.B. Purcell, Richmond, was chairman of the Entertainment Committee. First, the opening day reception was held at the Jefferson; carriage tours were available the next day, visiting the historic sights of the city. Then there was a James River trip to Jamestown, Old Point Comfort, and back from Newport News by train to Richmond.

Colonial Hotel, originally named the Green Hotel, was the first home of The National Bank.

Colonial Hotel, originally named the Green Hotel, was the first home of the National Bank of Blacksburg, organized in 1891.

PART FIVE

Three Decades of Great Change—1900-1930

1

Economic Panics—The Curse of Instability

"You are all familiar with the condition—panic—it can come without reason, and without warning ...."
—VBA President George J. Seay, 1902

VIRGINIANS JOINED OTHER AMERICANS in saying goodbye to the 19th century, many happy to see it fade into history. From the beginning of banking in the Old Dominion there had been ongoing struggles to establish a solid economic base. Periods of economic stringency, the advent of hostilities, political and social upheaval and the fear of economic domination by banks had all tended to restrain progress.

A glance back shows that prior to 1863, bank panics were mostly attributable to demands that bank notes be converted to coin. After the Civil War the public started accepting national bank notes. While their acceptance improved, the notes were still plagued by the inability of banks to easily issue more of them when the supply was tight.

Free silver was an emotional issue by 1895. Led by William Jennings Bryan, a 36-year-old Nebraska congressman, advocates of free silver believed that silver was the monetary solution to the problems of farmers and other workers who felt they were oppressed by those who favored the gold standard. Bryan's oratory at the Democratic Convention in Chicago gave him the party nomination for President in 1896. Republicans took the other side of the argument and nominated William McKinley, a strong advocate of the gold standard. In the election, McKinley prevailed, receiving 271 electoral votes to Bryan's 176. The 1900 con-

Entire staff of Arlington Trust Company, Arlington, circa 1914.
(Courtesy Arlington Trust Company)

test was a rerun of the 1896 election, and this time McKinley was reelected by an even larger margin. With McKinley's support, passage of the Currency Act of 1900 put the nation on the Gold Standard.

When representatives of bankers associations from Virginia, North Carolina and Georgia gathered in Savannah, June 17-19, 1902, for the first Interstate Banking Convention, one of the chief topics for discussion was how to deal with economic panics. In this historic session the Virginia Bankers Association's delegation was headed by George J. Seay, cashier of the Petersburg Savings and Insurance Company, of Petersburg.

"The quesiton of currency and banking reform ... is the most serious commercial problem now before the American people," Seay told his colleagues. "Every panic works a readjustment of the country's wealth and usually transfers it from weak to strong hands." He quoted a prominent New York banker: "This country is without a bank of ultimate reserve. There is no reservoir of cash to which any of those dispensing credit may go when in need. It is the one glaring defect in our banking system."

"The question of currency and banking reform ... is the most serious commercial problem now before the American people."

The three state banking associations at the conference convened separately for their business sessions. The VBA convention—the Ninth Annual—met on a hot Wednesday morning in the gentleman's parlor of the De Soto Hotel in Savannah. In attendance at that meeting, according to the roll call, were only 23 banker-delegates from the VBA.

How did this historic meeting come about?

Incoming President Oliver J. Sands, head of American National Bank in Richmond and chairman of the VBA Executive Committee, reported on its genesis. Said Sands, "The matter of holding a joint meeting, suggested by the North Carolina Bankers Association at its meeting in Asheville, entailed considerable work upon the Committee, as approval of the suggestion had to be approved by each member of the Committee, as well as the consent of the Lynchburg bankers on account of our Association having previously accepted their invitation."

Sands said a joint committee met in Charlotte in August 1901 and again in February to work out details.

At the VBA Convention business session, O.J. Sands was elected President. N.P. Gatlin of Lynchburg was named secretary, and H.A. Williams of Richmond was elected treasurer. Also elected were nine vice presidents, one from each of the VBA Districts.

A significant action took place at the VBA Convention, marking early on that the Virginia association was willing to take a stand on the issue of currency reform, one that was fraught with controversy at the time.

The delegates got the ball rolling for better currency control by adopting the following resolution: "Be it resolved, That it is the belief of the Virginia Bankers Asssociation that some changes in the present banking laws of this country should be made during this period of great prosperity, that will make the currency of the country more responsive to the needs of the commercial interests and that would minimize the recurrence of panics and money stringency; be it

"Resolved, That the Senators and Representatives in Congress of the State of Virginia be requested to give these questions most earnest thought and energetically give to us their efforts to have passed at an early day some bill that will so improve the present currency system as to make it better meet the requirements of trade at all seasons."

A memorable time was had in Savannah in 1902. The delegates had been welcomed graciously to the city, reminded at the outset, "No time lock runs against your stay with us, and no drastic regulation banishes you home after banking hours. The three days of grace shall be extended by local enactment, and the penalties which usually `fit the crime' even in this liberal city shall be suspended," spoke Pleasant A. Stovall, editor of the *Savannah Press.*

The meeting over, Virginia bankers boarded their trains and headed for the Old Dominion, sharing with North Carolina and Georgia that the new century would bring many challenges and changes to banking.

2

Major Issue—A Central Bank

"There is no subject upon which the human mind has more exercised itself than upon the subject of currency."
—U.S. Senator John W. Daniel, of Virginia, at the 1903 VBA Convention in Lynchburg

THE PANIC OF 1907 began on March 13. Banking was outdated and desperately in need of major reform—that was the opinion of many bankers in Virginia and the nation. This was a major theme for discussion by VBA Conventions of that day. The serious financial panics in 1873, 1884, 1893, 1903 and 1907 had heightened interest in currency control. As Senator John Daniel had told the bankers in Lynchburg in 1903, the subject of money was always on the minds of people.

President William McKinley died on September 14, 1901, after being shot by an assassin in Buffalo on September 6. The gold-based prosperity of the early 1900s had turned the sights of the country upward. But nothing much was done about the nation's financial structure. Vice President Theodore Roosevelt became chief executive upon McKinley's death.

Roosevelt tackled the "money trusts" but did very little to press for monetary reform. Congress also did very little. The lack of a central banking system resulted in economic shocks that could have been avoided. The tragic San Francisco earthquake of 1906 spread a measure of apprehension across the country, and some financial lenders talked in terms of the nation's economic equilibrium being destroyed.

The year—1905—The Occasion—Virginia Bankers Association Convention Reception at Lakeside Country Club, Richmond.

In the summer of 1907 the New York Stock Exchange faced a panic, and as the panic spread, eight New York banks failed in October. The timing of the collapse caught one of Wall Street's powerful financial leaders, J.P. Morgan, in Richmond, where he was attending an annual conference of the Episcopal Church. Morgan was forced to return to New York, where he and other leading bankers, along with U.S. Treasury officials, were able to keep the period of money stringency fairly short. The panic's impact was not serious to Virginia bankers, for the most part, but it served as further proof that the cycle of fear was increasingly dangerous.

The existing system of three so-called reserve cities—New York, Chicago and St. Louis—highlighted the debate over whether a central bank should be created. National banks in these cities collected funds from smaller regional banks. This formed large pools of deposits, but the money was being used for speculative investments by the reserve city banks. Sometimes it was difficult for regional banks to call their deposits. Check clearing and collecting on out-of-town banks were often long delayed.

By 1907, 95 percent of the business of the nation was transacted by credit instruments, five percent by cash. Maintaining the equilibrium of the credit fabric was no easy task.

Advocates of improved marketing and advertising techniques thought that banking's use of promotion "conveys the idea that Noah's ark is still the model for pleasure yachts, and that powdered wigs and velvet breeching are yet the mold of fashion. Banking is tough." Bankers were urged to heed their mission to "charm the reluctant dollar from the stockings of the fearful and add to the sums that work together for the development of the industrial and commercial interests of the country."

After President Teddy Roosevelt decided to seek currency control legislation, he turned to Senator Nelson W. Aldrich of Rhode Island and Representative Charles N. Fowler of New Jersey, chairmen of the finance committees in their respective bodies. Each submitted bills. The Currency Committee of the American Bankers Association favored the Fowler bill. Nothing happened. Representative Edward B. Vreeland of New York then advanced a bill which permitted the circulation of currency based on bonds, separate from those of the federal government, and commercial paper. Populists viewed these proposals with a wary eye, and progressives from the more industrially-developed areas feared any effort for the centralization of political and economic power.

As the 1908 election was approaching, public pressure grew on Congress and the Roosevelt administration to take steps to eliminate the causes of the previous year's panic. Reacting to this, Congress passed a modified bill on May 30, known as the Aldrich-Vreeland measure, or the Currency Law of 1908. It permitted the emergency issue of currency against the deposits of government and other obligations, including commercial paper guaranteed by national bank "associations" to be formed under the law. However, the most long-run value of the law was to create the National Monetary Commission to thoroughly study the banking problem.

In 1911 the Commission's report was filed. The Aldrich Plan, as it came to be called, provided for a National Reserve Association made up of member banks throughout the country to have a paid-in capital of $100 million. Its headquarters would be in Washington, with the nation divided into 15 districts, each district to have a branch. The Association would issue currency based on gold and commercial paper, not to be the liability of the federal government.

The bill was quickly developed, introduced in the Senate in 1912, where it died for lack of support. It was a victim of agrarian opposition as well as other critics who said it favored the larger banks.

The political climate was changing, however, and the election of 1910 created a Democratic Congress. That changed matters, as the new leaders would occupy center stage in 1911.

Bankers from Virginia had gone to Denver for the 1908 ABA Convention. Woodrow Wilson, native of Staunton, Virginia, was then Governor of New Jersey, and had been invited to address the annual convention. Speaking on the subject "The Banker and the Nation," the future President asked, "Where and whose is the money of the country? Bankers can answer the question, but I have met very few of them who could answer it in a way the ordinary man could understand."

He praised the bankers for their expertise in specialized knowledge of economic facts and industrial circumstances "of which they are masters in an extraordinary degree." He concluded his short address with the observation that many bankers are "singularly indifferent about what I may call the social functions and the political functions of banking, particularly in a country governed by opinion." The bankers listened, for they reckoned that the native Virginian was a rising political figure who was interested in monetary reform.

3

Virginia's Carter Glass and the Federal Reserve

"Why use dynamite when insect powder will do?"
—Rep. Carter Glass, debating his bill for the Federal Reserve System in 1913

CARTER GLASS, A NEWSPAPER PUBLISHER AND EDITOR from Lynchburg, is generally credited with being the "father of the Federal Reserve System."

Born on January 4, 1858, the five-foot-four Glass worked his way to the top rung of statemanship and established a leadership role in monetary and currency reform through the creation of the Federal Reserve.

When Glass died on May 28, 1946, he had served for 26 years as U.S. Senator from Virginia. He also had been Secretary of the Treasury under Woodrow Wilson (1918-1920) and prior to that he was a U.S. Representative from Virginia from November 4, 1902, until December 16, 1918, when he resigned to accept the cabinet appointment.

He was interested in monetary reform from the time he became a member of Congress in 1902. A Democrat, he later became chairman of the House Committee on Banking and Currency. As his leadership power increased, he was chosen to lead the Virginia delegation in support of Wilson.

Shortly after the defeat of the Aldrich Bill, Glass was named to head a subcommittee of the Banking and Currency Committee. The subcommittee was given the task of framing the necessary legislation for banking and currency reform. Glass observed that the technical nature of the assignment and the lack of information by individual members was a problem. He turned to Dr. H. Parker Willis, a former professor of economics at Washington and Lee University. An acknowledged expert on banking and finance matters because of his previous

Virginia's Carter Glass provided the leadership for the Federal Reserve.

work with the House Ways and Means Committee, Professor Willis was the Washington representative of the New York *Journal of Commerce* when he agreed to assist Glass. They shared kindred views.

Governor Wilson, campaigning for the Democratic nomination, had assured the people that his administration would do something about banking reform.

Glass and his subcommittee worked all summer, and by October 1912 the tentative draft of the elements of the bill were finished. After Wilson's election, Glass made an appointment with the President-elect at his home in Princeton on December 26, 1912. He left Lynchburg on Christmas Day for the train trip with Dr. Willis to discuss the proposals with Wilson.

When they arrived in Princeton there was two feet of snow on the ground, but Glass and Willis kept the appointment.

When they arrived in Princeton there was two feet of snow on the ground, but Glass and Willis kept the appointment. They found Wilson in his bedroom, propped up on two pillows, suffering from a bad cold. Despite his illness, he was anxious to discuss the proposal. To indicate his interest, Wilson had canceled all other appointments to devote more time to his visitors from Virginia.

Governor Wilson learned that the Glass proposal would remedy the inelastic money supply, and that it provided for the establishment of 20 or more privately-controlled regional reserve banks. When Wilson suggested a central board to be a public rather than the banker-controlled proposal of the Aldrich plan, Glass felt more comfortable, for he had opposed the Aldrich measure.

This historic meeting put together the general shape of the legislation, although much work remained to be done. To refine the concept Wilson later met with Glass, Secretary of the Treasury William G. McAdoo, and Senator Robert Owen of Oklahoma, the chairman of the newly-established Senate Committee on Banking and Currency.

It is an interesting fact that Senator Owen was also a native Virginian. He was born on February 2, 1856, in Lynchburg, practiced law in Virginia, and moved to Oklahoma, where he was the founder of the First National Bank of Muscogee in 1890. When Oklahoma was admitted to the Union in 1907, Owen was elected as a Democrat to the United States Senate. He had developed his own proposal for legislation, different from the Glass-Wilson proposal, but later became a patron of the Glass bill. He died on July 19, 1947, and was buried in Spring Hill Cemetary in Lynchburg, where Carter Glass had been buried the previous year.

President Wilson addressed a joint session of Congress on June 23, 1913, outlining his program for currency reform. Bankers in the money centers—the old reserve cities of New York, Chicago and St. Louis—were chilled by the proposals. They feared political control of the system. William Jennings Bryan and his liberal supporters thought the proposal gave too much power to bankers, and some national bank leaders thought the compulsory membership feature was severe.

Newspapers joined the fracus. *The New York Sun,* for example, portrayed the bill as "this preposterous offspring of ignorance and unreason ... covered all over with the slime of Bryanism."

In an attempt to placate the opposition within the banking industry, Wilson, Glass, Owen and McAdoo met with the ABA's Currency Commission. The meeting resulted in some modifications, but lingering critics remained who saw in the proposal political rather than banker control of the board. Wilson stuck to his view, but did agree to a compromise to permit the bankers to select a Federal Advisory Council to meet with the board to exert some influence through exchange of ideas.

Bryan, then Secretary of State, insisted that the Federal Reserve notes should be the obligations of the federal government. President Wilson told Glass that the bill should be changed to provide that, but Glass protested strenuously. The diminutive Virginian reminded President Wilson of the fact that the note issues were so well secured that the chance of government obligation was remote.

Wilson is quoted as saying, "Exactly so, Glass .... Every word you say is true; the government liability *is* a mere thought. And so, if we can hold to the substance of the thing and give the other fellow the shadow, why not do it, if thereby we may save our bill."

Alternate porposals threatened the bill. It was a very frustrating experience for Chairman Glass. It is said that at one time Glass was so exasperated that he threatened to resign. Replied Wilson, "Damn it, don't resign old fellow; outvote them!"

Not famed for his patience, Glass became disgusted with the tactics of his opponents when he had to present his bill to the Democratic Caucus. Some of his listeners noted that Glass showed a "fighting spirit." Someone yelled, "Give 'em hell, Carter."

He replied, "Why use dynamite when insect powder will do?" After heated debate, the Federal Reserve Bill was passed in the House on September 18 by a large majority, 287-85. It had a more difficult time in the Senate, but it prevailed by a vote of 54-34.

The Federal Reserve Act became a law a few hours after its passage on December 24, 1913.

The Federal Reserve Act became a law a few hours after its passage on December 24, 1913.

President Wilson signed the bill at the White House. At 6 p.m. he walked into his office, looked at the people present, but did not at first see Carter Glass at the far end of the room. He invited his fellow-Virginian to sit beside him at the table.

It was a perfect Christmas gift for President Wilson. Historians say that it was the most significant accomplishment of the first administration of President Wilson.

Glass, writing in 1935, said: "Next to my own family, the Federal Reserve System is nearest to my heart."

CONSENSUS MAKING ROLE OF THE VBA

The Glass-Owen Currency Bill was the urgent business of a called meeting of the Virginia Bankers Association, held at the Hotel Richmond on September 27, 1913. Bankers from as far away as Abingdon and Wytheville attended the daylong session that was presided over by President Joseph M. Hurt of Blackstone.

The VBA's Executive Council called the meeting to hear a report about what had taken place in Chicago on August 22 at a gathering of the presidents of the state bankers associations, clearing house leaders, and others. The meeting in Chicago was attended by representatives of 47 state bankers associations, including the VBA. President Hurt was represented by O.J. Sands of Richmond, a former VBA president.

At the special meeting on September 27, the first order of business was a vote that declared the day-long proceedings to be an executive session for full and free discussion of the important matter of currency control.

"First, I want to call your attention to the fact that both the Republican and Democratic parties are committed to banking and currency reform. Whether we get it now or sometime later, whether we get it to suit us or not, it is sure to come," President Hurt said.

Hurt argued that the existing banking and currency systems had not measured up in times of stress to the necessities of trade. He pointed out the problem of moving crops to market each year without a stronger currency. He also mentioned the need for more rural credit.

"Let us put aside all prejudice and selfishness and try to arrive at conclusions that will do us honor as Virginia bankers," the leader urged.

A resolution was offered by Sands for discussion later on: "Whereas, The Virginia Bankers Association has repeatedly and for years urged upon its representatives in Congress to favor the enactment of such laws as would correct the many defects in our present Banking and Currency system; and

"Whereas, The present Democratic administration is the only administration which has taken up the subject with the earnestness which insures the country such relief and the benefits which a proper system will give; and

"Whereas, In the opinion of the Virginia Bankers Association it is the honest purpose of the administration to enact laws which are for the benefit of the people, and are willing to hear and consider comments and suggestions from those who are experienced and equally honest and sincere in their desire to have enacted a law which will be workable and fair to all; and, therefore, be it

"Resolved, That the Glass-Owen Bill in its general scope and plan will give the country a much improved system ...."

The resolution then presented suggestions for changes in the bill, including the phasing in of the 12 banks; required that capitalization of the reserve banks should be reduced to $2,500,000; the shareholders should have at least minority representation on the board; the notes issued by the Federal Reserve Banks should be the obligations only of the banks.

The object of the lobbying on the bill, they agreed, should be directed to Virginia Senators Thomas S. Martin and Claude A. Swanson, as the House had already passed the bill.

President Hurt spoke at length, saying, "Some bill is going to be passed, and I advise you gentlemen not to be moderate in your demands. You need not bend the knee to any man. I say whether New York says one thing, or Chicago says another, be men enough to ask what you think is right, not influenced by anybody, but think as Virginians, and whether you stand or fall maintain your independence and the heritage of your fathers whose blood flows through you."

The convention delegates applauded. After a luncheon at the Jefferson Hotel, hosted by the Richmond banks, the Resolutions Committee reported. Several suggestions were added. One specifically said that the bill ... "in its present shape, is inequitable, especially to national banks, in forcing them to become members ... or else give up their charters, the State banks being given the privilege of joining or retiring from the Reserve Association at their option ...."

The Resolutions were adopted, and the special meeting was adjourned.

Virginia's Congressional Delegation and The Vote on the Glass Bill in 1913

U.S. Senate—Thomas S. Martin, Charlottesville, Yes
Claude A. Swanson, Chatham, Yes

U.S. House—William A. Jones, Warsaw, Yes
Edward E. Holland, Suffolk, Yes
Andrew J. Montague, Richmond, Yes
Walter A. Watson, Jennings Ordinary, Yes
Edward W. Saunders, Rocky Mount, Yes
Carter Glass, Lynchburg, Yes
James Hay, Madison, Yes
Charles Carlin, Alexandria, Yes
C. Bascom Slemp, Big Stone Gap, No
Henry D. Flood, Appomatox, Yes

During the course of the debates in 1913, spells of great oratory with a touch of caustic humor came forth. In the Senate on December 23—just before the favorable vote on the conference report—the opponents of the Glass-Owen Bill were making a "whipping boy" out of one of their own, Senator Joseph L. Bristow, Progressive Republican from Kansas. One of his colleagues taunted Bristow with this:

"I remember, Mr. President, that somewhere in the sacred songs we hear in the revival services there is something like this:

'There is a fountain filled with blood
Drawn from Immanuel's veins;
And sinners plunged beneath that flood
Lose all their guilty stains.'

"Mr. President, I fancy I can hear the distinguished Senator from Kansas in his new conversion improvising and paraphrasing that ... his new chant to be:

'There is a fountain filled with gold
Drawn from corporate veins;
And if I can be gathered into its fold
I may lose my Progressive stains.'"

Laughter followed. The Senate passed the bill.

At the VBA Convention held at Hotel Chamberlin, Old Point Comfort, June 17-19, 1915, W.B. Vest, of Newport News, announced that the VBA had 358 members. "I was present at the meeting of the Virginia bankers held in Richmond in 1893, at which 46 persons were present, and the Virginia Bankers formally launched," he said.

Bankers hoped that the time of the economic panics had passed. But war had broken out in Europe. "Little did we think when we met last year on this delightful spot that before this meeting practically the whole world would be at war and we ourselves trembling on the brink. It is horrible beyond conception and no man knoweth the limits to be reached, or can foretell its results," President Vest said.

4

Richmond Gets Fifth District Fed

"The fact that Richmond, already known to our people, knows their needs, knows the condition of our crops, knows the character of our people, so there need be no delay, not only in the shipping of currency back to us, but in passing on our paper."

—J.C. Brown, Raleigh banker, speaking for the N.C. Bankers Association for Richmond's application

AFTER ENACTMENT OF THE FEDERAL RESERVE legislation, no time was lost by the various regions throughout the nation to get a branch.

Richmond was selected as the Fifth District Federal Reserve Bank location after a well-coordinated campaign. The Richmond committee represented 13 local organizations, and Baltimore's chief proponent was the Merchants and Manufacturers Association.

The law provided that the Secretary of the Treasury, the Secretary of Agriculture and the Comptroller of the Currency were to constitute the Reserve Bank Organization Committee. They were to hold hearings and "to designate not less than eight nor more than twelve cities to be known as Federal Reserve cities." Their recommendations were not subject to review "except by the Federal Reserve Board."

The Organization Committee's hearing for the Baltimore-Washington applications were heard in Washington on January 6, 1914. The presentation for Richmond centered on the city's geographical location, as well as its communications, business, banking and trade connections. Another major factor was the active support for Richmond from the North Carolina Bankers Association and the South Carolina Bankers Association. Naturally, the Virginia Bankers Association put its shoulder to the wheel to help develop support.

The North Carolina Bankers Association filed a brief with the Federal Reserve Organization Committee, "expressing a strong preference for Richmond," and stating that it was "unquestionably the city" best qualified to serve the region.

(Courtesy Federal Reserve Bank of Richmond)

NCBA President George Holderness of Tarboro presented his organization's viewpoint to the committee.

Treasury Secretary McAdoo, chairman of the selection committee, asked Holderness, "Is it your observation that the course of trade is with Richmond, instead of Baltimore?"

"Absolutely, sir," Holderness replied. Many others spoke for Richmond, including J. Elwood Cox, a High Point banker, who said, "I think Richmond is the only city that could be familiar with the three great lines in North Carolina, cotton, peanuts, and tobacco."

And Colonel John F. Bruton, a Wilson banker, observed, "I feel like we would be a little away from home to take us to Baltimore."

Results of a survey of the banks in the states covered showed Richmond the preference over Baltimore by a vote of 167 to 128. It was noted that each state preferred one of its own cities with the exception of North Carolina, where all the votes were for Richmond.

When the committee released its final decision on April 2, 1914, Baltimore was shocked. Criticism was rampant, so much so that the committee released its reasons for favoring Richmond on April 10. Some of the justification included the nearness of Baltimore to Philadelphia; the conclusion that Richmond was more closely associated with the proposed district than Baltimore; and the fact that North Carolina, South Carolina and Virginia bankers preferred Richmond.

Although Baltimore continued to ask for reconsideration, nothing happened to change the location of the Fifth District Federal Reserve Bank in Richmond. However, Baltimore was given early consideration for a branch in that city. It was approved, and was opened for business by March 1, 1918. Charlotte was the second city to request a branch. Action for it developed in the two Carolinas in 1921. It was approved and opened on December 1, 1927. Hugh Leach of Richmond became the first head of the Charlotte Branch and later President of the Federal Reserve Bank of Richmond.

In May 1914, after raising more than the $4 million capital stock subscriptions from the agreeing national banks, the Organization Committee named the following banks to execute the certificate of incorportion: Merchants and Mechanics National Bank, Baltimore; First National Bank, Roanoke; Citizens National Bank, Charleston; Palmetto Natonal Bank, Columbia; and the Murchison National Bank, Wilmington.

The representatives of the five banks met on May 18, 1914, in the directors' room of the First National Bank, Richmond, to execute a Certificate of Organization. This certificate was transmitted to John Skelton Williams, the Comptroller of the Currency. Williams, a Richmond businessman who had been appointed comptroller earlier in the year by President Wilson, moved swiftly to commission the Federal Reserve Bank of Richmond and see that it was authorized to open for business.

The law required that the bank have nine directors, divided equally into three classes, A, B and C.

The first directors chosen were: Waldo Newcomer, Baltimore; Colonel J.F. Bruton, Wilson; Edwin Mann, Bluefield; George J. Seay, Richmond; D.R.

Coker, Hartsville; and James F. Oyster, Washington. Directors named by the Federal Reserve Board were: William Ingle, Maryland, chairman of the board and Federal Reserve Agent; James A. Moncure, Virginia, deputy chairman and deputy Federal Reserve Agent; and M.F.H. Gouverneur, of North Carolina.

Meeting on October 15, 1914, George J. Seay, Richmond, was elected the first governor of the Federal Reserve Bank of Richmond.

The Virginia Bankers Asssociation remembered with pride that Governor Seay (later—1936—the title changed to president) was president of the VBA in 1901-02, and had spoken eloquently about the need for currency control to prevent economic panics. A long time had intervened between the destruction of the Second Bank of the United States by Jackson's veto in 1832 and the creation of the Federal Reserve System by a Virginia leadership group, headed by Woodrow Wilson and Carter Glass. Now the nation had a central bank and Virginia was the home of one of 12 regional banks, thanks in part to the efforts of the VBA.

Heads of the Fed in Richmond

George J. Seay, October 5, 1914, through February 29, 1936
Hugh Leach, March 12, 1936, through February 28, 1961
Edward A. Wayne, March 1, 1961, through March 31, 1968
Aubrey N. Heflin, April 1, 1968, through January 16, 1973
Robert P. Black, August 6, 1973, through December 31, 1992
J. Alfred Broaddus, January 1, 1993—

Seay, of course, had served as president of the Virginia Bankers Association, and Wayne was a former managing officer of the North Carolina Bankers Association from 1940 to 1943.

Writing in the Annual Report of the Richmond Fed in 1989, James Parthemos, Senior Vice President and Director of Research, noted that the group managing the campaign to bring the Fed Bank to Richmond had worked for three months.

"The chief architect of that campaign was George J. Seay," Parthemos wrote. It was his oral presentation in Washington and his brief that had put Richmond in a good position for favorable consideration. Seay, with other Richmond leaders, had gone through the Carolinas to mobilize bankers and business leaders to support Richmond. The selection on April 2, 1914, "was a great personal triumph."

Seay was a native of Petersburg where he was born in March 1862. He won first honors upon graduation from high school and accepted employment as a runner at Petersburg Savings and Insurance Company at age 17. He rose through the ranks to cashier. In 1909, seven years after he had been elected President of the VBA, Seay resigned from Petersburg Savings to join the Richmond brokerage firm of Scott & Stringfellow. An early supporter and student of banking and currency reform, Seay followed the progress of the legislation to create the Federal Reserve in Congress with great interest. On December 28, 1913, he was employed by the Committee on Locating a Federal Reserve Bank in Richmond to put together its case.

Parthemos also wrote that newspapers credited Virginia Governor William

George J. Seay, first head of the Federal Reserve Bank of Richmond, was a former president of the VBA. Seay served as Governor of the Fed until 1936.
(Photo courtesy Federal Reserve Bank of Richmond)

Hodges Mann "with the initial suggestion that an effort be made to locate a reserve bank in Richmond." He wrote a letter dated December 2, 1913, to Oliver J. Sands, "prominent Richmond banker," and suggested that Richmond might well be a good place for the bank. Sands, also a former President of the Virginia Bankers Association (1902-03), had followed Seay in that top office and had helped arouse interest in the reserve bank for Richmond.

On the front page of the *News Leader* of December 17, 1913, a three-column headline said: "Reserve Bank To Be Sought Here."

At a special meeting of bankers held at the Business Men's Club in Richmond on Monday afternoon, December 29, forward movement began. Parthemos

Federal Reserve Bank of Richmond at Ninth and Franklin, groundbreaking on June 2, 1919.
(Courtesy Federal Reserve Bank of Richmond.)

points out that the local banking community "had quite suddenly upgraded Richmond's chances." Sands served as Chairman of the meeting, for it was felt that insufficient enthusiasm for the chances of getting a reserve bank had been evident up to the time when Sands and Seay became involved.

Other groups and leaders became involved in what Parthemos describes as "a campaign remarkable for its unbridled American booster spirit and for its effectiveness in putting together a convincing case in a brief span of time."

Doris E. Harless, also of the Fed, wrote in 1989 that the Federal Reserve Bank of Richmond opened at 9 a.m. on Monday, November 16, 1914, at 1109 East Main Street in a building formerly occupied by the City Bank of Richmond. World War I delayed construction of a new building until 1919 at Ninth and Franklin. As space was needed, additions were made. In 1970, a seven-acre site on the north bank of the James River was secured, and in August 1973 a new 26-story high rise at 701 East Byrd Street became the headquarters.

The Federal Reserve Bank of Richmond opened at 9 a.m. on Monday, November 16, 1914, at 1109 East Main Street.

5

World War I—Patriotism and Performance

"... the world now knows that the wealth of America, as well as its manhood, is marshaled today beneath the Stars and Stripes; that there are no conscripts, but all are eager volunteers."

—VBA President E.B. Spencer, Roanoke, speaking at the Twenty-Fourth Annual Convention, June 21, 1917, Old Point Comfort

VIRGINIANS, NOT UNLIKE OTHER AMERICANS, hoped that war would never come. Although hostilities had been raging in Europe since August 1914, President Woodrow Wilson stressed neutrality. America was unprepared.

But war did come to the United States on April 6, 1917, after Wilson delivered his war address to Congress.

The VBA Convention that year convened at the Hotel Chamberlin at Old Point Comfort. Speaking at the first session in the hotel ballroom, Roanoke banker E.B. Spencer, the association's president, expressed the gravity of the day. Said he, "Little did we think, when we met here just twelve months ago, at this 'clearing house of hospitalities,' that our next meeting would find our nation shadowed by the sorrow that duty to humanity had called to the stern tasks of war."

President Spencer pledged that "cost what it may in blood and treasure, our sword shall not be sheathed until governments of humanity, by humanity, and for humanity shall spread their wings above mankind throughout all the earth"

In his eloquent address, President Spencer pledged that "cost what it may in blood and treasure, our sword shall not be sheathed until governments of humanity, by humanity, and for humanity, shall spread their wings above mankind through all the earth."

The Secretary of the Treasury, Willam G. McAdoo, had called for the "stupendous loan" of two billion dollars, and immediately the banks, large and small, made tender of their services to the government, renouncing all claim to compensation or reimbursement for expense or trouble, and the response was overwhelming.

Also urgent was food production for the world. "Food, more food, and again more food with which to win the war," he said was the new "Battle Cry of the Republic."

The Twenty-Fifth VBA Convention held its meeting at Old Point Comfort, June 20-22, 1918. W.M. Addison, a Richmond banker, was president. He noted the Silver Anniversary and the VBA's "constructive work" since its founding in 1893, and "distinguished rank among the public agencies of conservatism and progress."

But the war was at its critical stage, and President Addison reviewed what had been done, saying, "The bankers of our State have been quick to take vigorous hold upon the obligations which have been presented and have given them adequate discharge ...."

He reported what had been accomplished for Liberty Bonds in the three Liberty Loan issues:

"Virginia in the first loan exceeded her maximum apportionment of $21,000,000 by nearly $5,000,000," he said.

Continuing the positive report, he noted that in the second loan drive, Virginia had exceeded her maximum of $45,000,000 by $5,800,000; the third loan, a maximum of $29,809,000, Virginia "had hit her stride and turned in subscriptions of $44,000,000 or $14,000,000 in excess." President Addison said that the energetic work of bankers and others was "sufficient evidence to Germany, I trust, that Virginia is organized and earnest in her determination, with her sister States, to win

Series 1918 two dollar bank note, Federal Reserve Bank of Richmond.
(Courtesy Federal Reserve Bank of Richmond.)

Delivering new bank vault to Farmers and Merchants National Bank building, Winchester, Virginia, 1917.

the fight for those principles which give us freedom and the right to govern ourselves in accordance with terms which this country shall alone dictate."

He pointed out that the establishment of the Federal Reserve prevented a very difficult financial situation in war financing that would have taken place under the former banking system. The Fifth Federal Reserve District exceeded its maximum allotment in each of the three loans.

"While the victory is being won, forget not that at the front, fighting for the cause of Liberty, are many of those heretofore active in our Virginia banks—our associates and our friends—erect, calmly poised and unafraid, they represent the greatest contribution this Association can make to the country's cause," he concluded.

The VBA Executive Council had met three times in 1917. One was on December 8, 1917, in Richmond, when it was decided "an intensive campaign would be inaugurated to induce every bank in Virginia to support our government in the sale of United States bonds and War Savings Certificates ...."

Secretary V. Vaiden, a Farmville banker, reported that the VBA had 403 member banks, which was the "largest in the history of our Association."

The matter of guaranteeing deposits in national banks, being considered by Congress, was opposed. A number of states had tried guaranty deposit legislation, and bankers found it unworkable in many places. The issue would arise again.

Victory came for the Allies on November 11, 1918. VBA President Garland E. Vaughan, of Lynchburg, observed at the Twenty-Sixth Annual Convention, June 19-21, at Old Point Comfort, "The world has for the four preceding years been plunged into the most horrible struggle the human race has ever experienced, and this great nation of ours, drawn reluctantly into the conflict, emerged not only conqueror, but has earned the gratitude of every right-thinking nation on earth." He enumerated Virginia's role in the victory. Final figures he reported for the Five Liberty Loans in Virginia totaled $264,412,350. Based on a population of 2,142,052, that gave the Old Dominion a per capita subscription of $123.42.

At hand was the task of readjustment to peace. One suggestion President Vaughn made to the bankers was to try to become leaders in the development of their respective communities. Thus, just as the Virginia bankers had met their responsibility in war, now they had to turn to the problems of inflation and recession.

At hand was the readjustment for peace.

6

The "Roaring Twenties"—Road to Disaster

"I am for economy. After that, I am for more econmy."
—President Calvin Coolidge, 1924

WORLD WAR I PROSPERITY CONTINUED TO 1920. Although agricultural prices declined after a whopping upsurge during the war, some economists believed that a reasonable contraction in the economy might aid the restoration of a more normal business environment.

It was a period of testing the newly created Federal Reserve System to determine its effectiveness to restrain credit abuses and to avoid the threat of boom and bust.

Speculation was the theme of the day!

The Eastville Bank, Eastville, Virginia, 1920

When the war ended it became apparent that the government had done little planning for demobilization. Soldiers returning home found few jobs in civilian life. Defense industries were closed or reduced. President Wilson, who had carried his native Virginia overwhelmingly in the elections of 1912 and 1916, was battling for his international plans. The Senate rejected the League of Nations and the treaty. Wilson, in ill health, lost his political grip. The momentum to pursue domestic matters suffered. During 1919 inflation rose by 77 percent; and in 1920, it increased another 28 percent.

Virginia still depended a great deal on good prices for agricultural commodities. In 1919 tobacco had reached 53 cents per pound; cotton brought 35 cents per pound. By 1926 cotton was below 12 cents; tobacco had dropped to the mid-twenties. When the major contraction began in the early 1920s, wholesale prices dropped 56 percent. The wild fluctuations concerned bankers over the quality of credit and loan portfolios. The Fed discount rate dropped from 7 percent in 1920 to a low of 4.5 percent in late 1921.

During the decade of the 1920s the miracle of radio made its appearance, providing instant contact to the world for both the city dweller and the farmer.

Vice President Calvin Coolidge became president when President Warren G. Harding died in 1923. A staunch advocate of economy and debt reduction, people seemed to like his austere approach, simplicity and basic honesty. John W. Davis, the Democratic nominee, carried Virginia by 62 percent over Coolidge in the 1924 election, but Coolidge carried the nation.

Henry Ford replaced the Model T with the Model A, and buggies were disappearing from the countryside. Electricity became available to an increasing number of households, and the number of tractors on Virginia farms increased.

A native of Winchester, Admiral Richard E. Byrd, became a national hero when he flew over the North Pole on May 9, 1926. On November 29, 1929, he flew over the South Pole.

In 1927, President Coolidge signed the McFadden Act, a so-called landmark law that prohibited national banks from branching in states where branching was prohibited to state banks.

A free-spirited attitude following the war produced the era of the flapper, bathtub gin and prohibition, burgeoning cities, and growth of crime, commentators declared.

Several states adopted anti-bank robber procedures. The Texas Bankers Association offered a $5,000 reward for **DEAD** bank robbers "legally killed while Robbing this bank." The Illinois Bankers Association set up a statewide vigilante campaign. The IBA alert to its members ended this way:

"A bank robber caught
Our work's not for naught;
A bank robber dead,
We're that much ahead."

The coming of the automobile made daylight robberies of banks more frequent as bandits could flee more easily.

But by 1928 bankers turned their attention to concerns in the money market. The stock market was closely monitored. Rates on commercial paper shot upward

But by 1928 bankers turned their attention to concerns in the money market.

each month, and money demand grew. The pressure forced Fed members to discount more heavily as demands for bank credit raised rates on all classes of money for business purposes and speculation.

Stock prices were moving up in 1923 and registered a 10 percent increase in 1924 and another 20 percent in 1925. By mid-1928, the Dow average had doubled, and by 1929—the peak—stock prices had risen another 50 percent. Speculation mania spread as stocks were easy to sell. As the securities business boomed, demand for commercial bank credit to finance stock purchases increased. Margin lending became rampant; bankers found themselves to be between the rock and a hard place as conventional loans decreased and the cost of money increased.

One of the top political stories in Virginia in the decade of the 1920s was the election of Harry Flood Byrd, who became Governor on February 1, 1926. In the presidential election of 1928, Virginia voted Republican, casting 53.9 percent of the vote for Herbert C. Hoover to 45.9 percent for Alfred E. Smith.

The nation was prosperous when Hoover became President in 1929. Call money rose to 20 percent in March. The discount rate was raised by the Fed to 6 percent, up from 3.5 percent.

The urge to get rich was overpowering. Roger Babson, noted Wall Street syndicated columnist, gave a chilling forecast: "There is a crash coming, and it may be a terrific one," but Wall Street and the nation were in no mood to listen to a gloomy prediction. Then came Black Tuesday, October 29, 1929, the day the bubble burst. It marked the beginning of the Great Depression.

PART SIX

Depression and the Roosevelt Era

1

Disarray in the Market Place

"The poorhouse is vanishing from among us."
—Herbert Hoover, 1928

THERE WAS INORDINATE DISARRAY in the market place when the frenzy of stock speculation came to an end in October 1929.

Even the conservative Hoover felt the excitement of the prosperous economy. In 1930 at the ABA Convention in Cleveland he said, "Our economic system is but an instrument of the social advancement of the American people. Any recession in American business is but a temporary halt in the prosperity of a great people."

And venerable Thomas A. Edison spoke on network radio in 1931: "Be courageous. I have lived a long time. I have seen history repeat itself, again and again. I have seen many depressions in business. Always America has come out stronger and more prosperous. Be as brave as your fathers were before you. Have faith. Go forward."

Virginians, having a tradition for conservatism and self-reliance, prepared to face the rising storm of economic turbulence. They braced for intensification of the downward trend. They had seen the foolhardy actions of the bullish way to hard times. Bankers had seen a deposit run-off by customers who heard the siren song of buy on margin.

Reports indicated that trading on the New York Stock Exchange on October 24, 1929, was a wild stampede. Some said it was "terrifying" as some brokers collapsed from the ordeal "and had to be carried from the floor."

The grave situation caused leading bankers to issue reassuring statements that finally checked the drop. Not since the panic caused by the war in 1914 had Wall Street seen such a dark and trying day.

The rapid stock market decline continued until mid-1932.

2

Banking Crisis—the Banking Holiday

"For three years prior to the moratorium the confidence of depositors was impaired by reason of the record of failures."
—VBA President S.W. Keys, of Glade Spring, at the Fortieth Annual Convention, Hot Springs, June 22, 1933

BAD NEWS GETS AROUND.

There was a diminishing supply of financial heroes and political leaders as the depression hit home in the 1930s. Henrik Ibsen is quoted as saying, "Those heroes of finance are like beads on a string—when one slips off, the rest follow."

Nevada was the first state to declare a statewide banking moratorium in October 1932. Very little front-page publicity was given to the act chiefly because there were only 20 banks in that state. However, as the bank runs began to develop, chiefly in the Midwest, the bad news got around.

The spreading problem reached maximum intensity in Michigan when Governor William A. Comstock, a former banker, responded to requests of bankers to declare a banking holiday for Valentine's Day, February 14, 1933. Other states followed in rapid sequence.

In the presidential ballot in Virginia in 1932, Virginia voted 68.5 percent of its votes for Franklin D. Roosevelt to 30.1 percent for Herbert C. Hoover, putting the Old Dominion in the Democratic column. Reports show that in July 1932 an estimated 19 percent of the total labor force of 148,000 workers in Virginia was unemployed.

The economic health of Virginia was far from robust, but the state did not suffer the ravage of depression as many other states did.

The economic health of Virginia was far from robust, but the state did not suffer the ravages of the depression as many other states did. This condition was attributed to the traditional conservatism—enhanced by the doctrine of Governor Byrd to "pay-as-you-go" and to stay out of debt. In previous times the state banks of Virginia had survived many national panics; no depositors lost their funds. The citizens of Virginia, when the 1930s arrived, did not have to carry heavy state and local debts. Businesses had been careful to avoid over-speculation. In short, Virginia could balance its budget. Governors John G. Pollard (1930-1934) and

George C. Perry (1934-1938), facing the severe years of the Great Depression, maintained a high degree of independence from the Roosevelt administration and the New Deal.

At the Fortieth Convention of the VBA in Hot Springs, June 22, 1933, President S.W. Keys, of Glade Spring, a small mountain town in Washington County, gave his address as head of the organization.

"Great things have happened since we last met together," he said at the time of the very depth of the depression.

To make the point, he told a good story. "In our section we have an old farmer who came to town some months ago on his usual Saturday afternoon visit to bring the gossip and to gather the news, and this was just after a very severe storm in his section. In reporting the storm to his friends he used every adjective he could recall to describe its severity, and its awfulness, and finally he reached the climax with this statement: 'Fellows, it was so awful that trees blew up that never blowed up before.' "

The delegates and guests at the convention understood when he said, "And things have happened since we last met which have never happened before."

In his chronicle of events, Keys reviewed the years 1932-1933, using vivid expressions to describe the conditions.

"Analysts and students of economic trends gave us bland assurances that the tide had turned. They were wrong. The cycle of depression had not ended. There were storms yet to weather, more severe than we had expected," he said.

"It has been a year literally crowned with economic and social changes, with governmental and political revolutions of far-reaching possibilities, and hurricanes which have swept over our financial structures, and left in their wake wreck and ruin .... On every hand there was the attitude of impatient waiting for something to happen. In this desperate situation our government appeared impotent to initiate reforms or adopt effective measures for relief," President Keys told the delegates at The Homestead.

"Anything that promised a change commanded a following. The psychology of the situation was that conditions could not be worse .... Party lines were forgotten in the extremity of economic necessity," he said.

"Tremendous is the responsibility resting upon those who assume to handle and protect the treasure of others .... We witnessed the spectacle of State after State declaring bank holidays. Confidence was gone, the nation was in panic. The greatest economic crisis of our history threatened. The first official act of our new President was to close every bank in the nation on March 6. That ended the panic. In a seizure of panic, people run with something, from something, toward something they fear less," he observed.

"In a seizure of panic, people run with something, from something, toward something they fear less," he observed.

To show that Virginia banks were not victims of the depression as in other states, he said, "The record of Virginia banks during the past year, comparatively speaking, is a source of some pride and gratification to us. On July 1, 1932, we had 248 State banks. On June 1, 1933, this number was 220, and during the period only four State banks were placed in receivership," he said.

"The VBA," Keys noted, "was born in the panic of 1893 .... In the four decades of its history it has been the articulate voice of the banks of Virginia. It has with-

Officers of the Virginia Bankers Association, 1940-1941. Left to right they are: Seated—Thomas H. Blanton, President, Bowling Green; G. Franklin Lenz, First Vice-President, Newport News; Standing—G. C. McCall, Second Vice-President, Norton; C. W. Beerbower, Secretary, Roanoke; (Giles H. Miller, Lynchburg, Past President, whose term of office expired at the 1940 Convention); Lillian A. Kendall, Assistant Secretary, Richmond; and Thomas D. Neal, Treasurer, Richmond. Made at VBA Convention in Roanoke, May 23-25, 1940.

stood both prosperity and adversity, panics and progress ... it should continue to serve us with increasing usefulness."

VBA Secretary C.W. Beerbower, a Roanoke banker, reported that for the year the association had lost 40 members, and that membership in 1933 was 410. The number was 574 in 1928, a peak year of prosperity. But Virginia had been more fortunate than many other states, Beerbower reported. Total income for the year was $10,328.02.

On Sunday night, March 5, the new President ordered a four-day National Banking Holiday, effective Monday, March 6, 1933.

Throngs of Democrats were in Washington for the inauguration of Franklin D. Roosevelt on Saturday, March 4, 1933. Visitors to the city were advised not to attempt to cash checks on out-of-town banks at the hotels. On Sunday night, March 5, the new President ordered a four-day national Banking Holiday, effective Monday, March 6, 1933.

FDR's order froze $40 billion of bank assets. His historic proclamation made use of a 1917 act that provided emergency powers for the president.

"Whereas there have been heavy and unwarranted withdrawal of gold and currency from the banking institutions for the purpose of hoarding," his order began, and "Whereas continuous and increasingly extensive speculative activity abroad in foreign exchange has resulted in severe drains on the nation's stock of gold ..." these conditions, according to President Roosevelt, "created a national emergency." He then summoned Congress to convene on Thursday, March 9.

Myron E. Bristow, Commissioner of Insurance and Banking, reported to the State Corporation Commission on December 31, 1933, that the banks in Virginia were closed on March 3. The Bank Holiday was later extended, using a schedule for banks in the 12 Federal Reserve cities to reopen on March 13. Member banks in cities with clearing houses would be permitted to open March 14. The other banks would fall in line for reopening, the sound banks to be promptly reopened. The banking departments of the states were asked to follow the same schedule.

In the first of many "fireside chats," FDR went on the radio on March 12. He had compliments for the citizenry for their patience during the banking holiday, and he stressed the role of banks in putting money to work for industry and agriculture.

"We do not want and will not have another epidemic of bank failures," he said.

Within a few days banking resumed serving its customers. Commissioner Bris-

Richmond Times-Dispatch

Richmond, Virginia, Monday, March 6, 1933

Roosevelt Orders 4-Day Holiday For All Banks, Forbids Outflow of Gold, Calls Congress Thursday; Checks and Credit Will Keep City Trade Flowing

Hitler Scores Sweep In German Elections On a New Reichstag

Cermak Fails; Death Is Seen In Few Hours

An Editorial
Real Democracy Again

City Prepares To Get Along Without Cash

'Scrip' For Trading Provided By Plans; Gold Basis Intact

Richmond Times-Dispatch

Richmond, Virginia, Wednesday, March 8, 1933

Federal Reserve Bank Frees Cash to Meet Payrolls And Food Movements Here; Meat Prices Increase

Soviet Spurns League Role In China War

Old Dominion Company Book, Tax Values Vary, Inquiry Witness Relates

U. S. Charges 6 in Denver Kidnap Case

Fresh Pork Leads Rise; Beef Follows

Text of Order Releasing Cash

Action Called Vital Step In Bank Holiday

Newspapers told their readers of the Banking Holiday on Monday Morning March 6, 1933, and subsequent actions.
(From A Century of Service)

tow listed 29 state banks in Virginia not permitted to reopen following the banking holiday for the year 1933. Of these, six were put in receivership, the report shows.

There were 238 state banks to start the year 1933; 203 were listed at the end of the year.

Banking's most critical year was 1933. ABA President Paul H. Sisson wrote in that fateful year: "So in the period of economic retraction and severe depression society sought its scapegoat and landed with remarkable unanimity upon the banker as the demon responsible for all their troubles .... Like all the people, he was caught in a tidal wave of general reaction, in which values of investments and collateral were wiped out in unbelievable volume and an economic law has worked its inexorable way with him quite as it has with other business."

3

Congress and the Alphabet Agencies

"Here's the bill. Let's pass it!"
—Chairman Henry B. Steagall,
House Banking Committee

PRESIDENT ROOSEVELT CALLED CONGRESS into special session March 9, 1933. Both Senate and House were strongly Democratic after the 1932 election. This assured quick passage of FDR's legislative agenda for the First Session of the Seventy-Third Congress.

Virginia was represented in the Senate by Carter Glass of Lynchburg and Harry Flood Byrd of Berryville, who had taken his seat on March 3 to fill the vacancy created by the resignation of Senator Claude A. Swanson of Chatham. House members were Clifton A. Woodrum of Roanoke, Andrew J. Montague of Richmond, Schuyler Otis Bland of Newport News, Thomas G. Burch of Martinsville, A. Willis Robertson of Lexington, Howard W. Smith of Alexandria, Patrick Henry Drewry of Petersburg, Colgate W. Darden, Jr., of Norfolk, and John W. Flannagan, Jr., of Bristol.

Heading the list for action was the Emergency Banking Bill, which had been developed by the administration. Since there had been no time for the bill to be printed, only a few people knew what it provided.

Chairman Henry B. Steagall of the House Committee on Banking and Currency, had the only copy. Upon entering the House chamber, the report goes, he waved the bill and shouted, "Here's the bill. Let's pass it!"

The National Recovery Act emblem of the New Deal displayed by industry and business.

The pressure was on. No amendments were permitted. After only 40 minutes of debate, the bill was passed.

Rushed to the Senate, the bill was passed within a few hours without change. It was the urgent action that Roosevelt wanted, and he signed it into law immedately. Some of its provisions were:

The bank holiday was legalized, and standards for reopening the banks were set. The Reconstruction Finance Corporation, created in the Hoover administration to provide a long list of monetary aids for business and industry, was strengthened. The RFC could invest in capital notes and preferred stock of banks where capital infusions were needed.

The government printing presses rolled as new Federal Reserve notes were authorized; new money began to circulate in Virginia and the country.

At a dizzy rate of speed in the first 100 days of the Roosevelt program, action turned out the so-called "alphabet agencies," including the Emergency Banking Act, Economy Act, Civilian Conservation Corps, Federal Emergency Relief Act, Agricultural Adjustment Act, Emergency Farm Mortgage Act, Tennessee Valley Authority Act, Truth-in-Securities Act, Glass-Steagall Banking Act and the Farm Credit Act.

The Glass-Steagall bill, the Banking Act of 1933, signed by Roosevelt on June 16, 1933, provided for the Federal Deposit Insurance Corporation. Several states had tried deposit guaranty insurance, going back to New York in 1829. Michigan had adopted a deposit insurance law in 1836, but it failed in 1842. Texas had a deposit guaranty law, but repealed it. Bankers—including the VBA— opposed deposit guarantee legislation. Senator Carter Glass, who was Chairman of the Senate Banking Committee in 1933, opposed it. Since 1886, some 150 proposals for deposit insurance had been made in Congress prior to 1933. Adamant that weak banks would drain the strong, President Roosevelt opposed it. Republican Senator Arthur H. Vandenberg was an avid supporter of deposit insurance. On March 10, 1933, he spoke on the subject in the Senate, repeating his request for action. Jesse Jones, RFC head, supported Vandenberg's efforts for action. He was a prominent Houston banker and newspaper publisher. With the concurrence of Vice President John Nance Garner, Vandenberg was able to get deposit guaranty insurance up for consideration as part of the pending banking bill. Roosevelt relented; the bill was modified to allow the FDIC to begin operations on July 1, 1934.

The U.S. Treasury contributed $150 million to the FDIC trust fund. Each of the 12 Federal Reserve Districts was to subscribe stock equal to one-half of its surplus as of January 1, 1933. Banks approved for membership were assessed an amount equal to one-half of one percent of insured deposits. The Banking Act of 1935 superseded the existing law. Changes included prohibition of payment of interest on demand deposits and limited the rate of interest paid on savings and time deposits, the famed "Regulation Q."

There seemed to be no end to legislation originating in Washington. Banking was covered by Social Security. Tax on employer and employee began at one percent from 1937 to 1939, escalated to three percent in 1949, which was said to be the absolute limit.

An odd twist for some bankers was the requirement for banks to set service charges and interest rates for all banking services. Each banking account, according to the theory, was to pay its own way. One banker is said to have quipped that it "was the first good hand that the banker has picked up in this new deal. It looks like four aces to us—let's play it hard."

The national debt was climbing—standing at $27 billion. Alarmed by the figure, Senator Glass said, "We need sound money .... I'm never going to vote for any greenbacks."

Virginia leadership began to resist the increase in Federal grants. They recalled that RFC's Jesse Jones had described Carter Glass as "the wisest of them all" on banking matters, and that Jones said: "Things nearly always get better if you give them time. That is particularly true with collateral and properties and people."

Virginians were relatively calm—and conservative—and they were pleased to assert that the Old Dominion way of doing things would lead them to a sound recovery.

Virginians were relatively calm—and conservative—and they were pleased to assert that the Old Dominion's way of doing things would lead to a sound recovery.

The full bloom of prosperity in the nation did not return until 1939 as defense spending for World War II stimulated a rapid recovery.

4

World War II-Financing the Arsenal of Democracy

"I attribute this fine result largely to the fact that in the Sixth [War Loan] the bankers of Virginia undertook the raising of this quota as their own particular responsibility."
—Dr. Francis P. Gaines, Chairman of the War Finance Committee, November 2, 1944

IN 1940, VIRGINIA BANKERS WERE STILL RECOVERING from the tenacious depression. As war raged in Europe—France fell to Germany, and Japan joined the Axis—the tempo of the march to conflict increased. Selective Service was adopted; Lend-lease passed Congress by a narrow margin in 1941. After Germany invaded Poland peace prospects collapsed.

World War II Ration Book Four gave bankers a headache in 1943 as the Office of Price Administration required that coupons had to be collected, counted and credited. The ration manual, bulky and complicated, was enough to give the bankers an "itchy rash," but the patriotic bankers managed.

On a quiet and mild Sunday afternoon, December 7, 1941, word came over the radio that the Japanese had bombed Pearl Harbor.

The war came to America. The surprise attack quickly united America, and all efforts were directed to victory. The banking industry once again was asked to lead financial efforts for defense. President Roosevelt told the nation that the estimated cost of the war through 1943 would be $83 billion.

Bankers realized that "wars are not won by armies and production alone. They are fought in the area of finance."

In one way or another, Virginians and Virginia bankers were off to war. Governor James Price named the Virginia Defense Council, the first state organization of its kind in the nation. Headed by the well-known historian and editor, Dr. Douglas Southall Freeman, it sought to ease the problems created by rapidly-expanding defense activities in Virginia. Around a half-million Virginians were in the armed forces in World War II, and 9,000 men and women from the state died in the service of their country.

Home front life was an existence with shortages of numerous things. Sugar, coffee, canned goods, meats, heating fuel, tires and gasoline were obtained by ration coupons and tokens. Drives for scrap metal, tin cans and waste paper were conducted. The home front had an elaborate civilian defense organization. At

The World War II photograph of a Norfolk public school classroom shows the intense patriotism on the homefront. Children recited the Pledge of Allegience. Victory gardens supplemented food shortages. Automobiles had "gone to war" as tanks and weapons were produced.
(Courtesy of the Library of Congress, Prints and Photographs)

every turn, people were asked to buy war bonds. Bankers, in addition to their other volunteer activities, were in the forefront of activities to support the financial effort for defense.

The VBA had joined in the effort through a wide variety of committees.

The VBA had joined in the effort through a wide variety of committees. A.E. Anderson, a Bristol banker, headed the VBA War Bond Committee in 1944. The Committee met at the John Marshall Hotel on November 2, following a Statewide Conference for the Sixth War Loan. In its issue of January 30, 1945, the *American Banker* published an article by Dr. Francis P. Gaines, President of Washington and Lee University, and volunteer Chairman of Virginia's War Finance Committee. His experience inspired the tribute to Virginia bankers.

The article called the work of Virginia bankers "outstanding." Anderson wrote, "I attribute this fine result largely to the fact that in the Sixth the bankers of Virginia undertook the raising of this quota as their own responsibility." The result that brought the commendations was "... the gratifying total of 151.8 percent."

In May 1944 the ABA had appointed Richmond banker W.A. Roper, as ABA War Loan Chairman for Virginia cooperation in War Loan work with banks. In July 1944, C.T. O'Neill, of Charlottesville, VBA president, appointed a War Bond Committee of the Association to assist the War Finance Committee. He named Bristol banker A.E. Anderson, Chairman, and named one banker from each of the VBA banking regions: Jack W. Nurney, Suffolk; R.H. Goode, Chase City; Harold G. Brown, Winchester; Giles H. Miller, Lynchburg; W.G. Waring, West Point; and R. Page French, Richmond.

Governor Colgate W. Darden named President O'Neill to the State Postwar Employment Committee as representative of all Financial Services in Virginia. Many other committees functioned for the VBA to take care of credit needs, such as the Virginia Bank Credit Group, headed by Richmond banker H. Hiter Harris. Nine of the larger Virginia banks had formed this group to make available $4,500,000 for small and medium-sized business in Virginia. Banker Joseph E. Healy, of Hampton, headed a committee on Re-Employment and Assistance to Veterans.

The Fifty-Second Annual Meeting of the VBA was set for The Homestead, Hot Springs, June 14-15, 1945.

In January 1945, the Office of Defense Transportation issued an order prohibiting all conventions or meetings attended by more that 50 persons. The VBA waited until April to see if the order might be modified, but the Executive Council had to announce that the meeting could not be held.

The decision was made and announced that a Special Meeting of the Executive Council to elect officers and the six members of the Executive Council would be proper. It was set for Wednesday, June 13, 1945, at the Hotel Richmond, Richmond, to begin at 10:30 a.m.

President Charles T. O'Neill presided. In his address, he reported on the war successes and "the successful though costly defeat of Germany." He noted the death of President Roosevelt on "the eve of European victory."

P.W. Anderson of Marshall was elected president. Joseph E. Healy of Hampton was elected first vice president; and Warren M. Goddard of Richmond, second vice president.

PART SEVEN

Market Forces and Financial Reform—1943-1993

1

Post-War Banking in Virginia

"Billions of bank credit for production, but not one cent for speculation."
—Secretary of the Treasury John Snyder

WITH THE DEFEAT OF GERMANY in May 1945, followed by the Japanese surrender in September, American veterans returned to their homes and jobs. The country was tired of war, proud of victory. Bank deposits had increased since wartime rationing had restricted the purchase of consumer goods.

The federal expenditure for World War II totaled $321.2 billion, ten times greater than the cost of World War I. Of that amount, about 41 percent came from current tax receipts. The rest came from borrowings through the banking system and bond purchases by individuals and others. Commercial banks bought about $78 billion of Government securities.

The banks emerged from World War II with assets over twice the pre-war total, while capital accounts were only about 25 percent larger.

From $49 billion in 1941, the national debt increased to $259 billion in 1945.

The ogre of inflation was a grave threat. To contain it, banking launched a major program to restrict inflation through cooperation with regulators to help dry up "the pool of consumer purchasing power and reduce speculation."

Consumer credit grew in the post-war years by leaps and bounds. By December 31, 1971, individual loans had reached 22.7 percent of all commercial bank loans.

The bank credit card—another form of consumer lending—gained widespread usage in the decade of the 1960s. Virginia banks not only joined the plastic card competition, but led it, with a major Virginia bank being one of the nation's pioneer card issuers.

Branch banking again became an issue in post-war Virginia. Branching laws at the time permitted banks to branch into major metropolitan areas of 50,000 population. Richmond banker Thomas C. Boushall was the strongest branching advocate of the day. The majority of the bankers, however, were opposed to branching. The VBA was called upon to act, and it petitioned the Assembly in 1948 to enact limitations. The Assembly responded with much more restrictive branching laws.

Branch banking again became an issue in post-war Virginia.

Branching remained an issue in the banking industry. There was no major new action in the Assembly again until the 1960s.

At the June 1960 Convention, R.C. deRosset of Lynchburg was elected VBA President. At his first Board meeting, he called for action that year on branching. At a later meeting, following a report from a special branching subcommittee, the Board voted to devote a main portion of the 1961 Convention to a debate and decision on branching, with proponents and opponents having equal time.

The Convention debate resulted in an approved resolution to appoint another study committee to conduct a "thorough and exhaustive study of branching laws" and report back to the 1962 Convention. The 1961 Convention failed in its attempt to adopt a firm position on the issue.

Washington, D.C.—May 21, 1953—Officials of Virginia Bankers Association meet with Board and Staff members of Federal Deposit Insurance Corporation.
Standing (l-r): Russell D. Miller, Vance L. Sailor, Forbes Campbell (all FDIC) J. O. Brett, General Counsel, American Bankers Association; Russell E. Shearer, Raymond D. Hengren and Edison Cramer (All FDIC).
Seated (l-r): Maple T. Harl, Director, FDIC; R. F. Burke Steele, President, Petersburg Savings & American Trust Co., Petersburg; Rawley F. Daniel, Secretary-Treasurer of the Virginia Bankers Association, Richmond; H. H. Cooley, Vice President, Round Hill National Bank, Round Hill; W. W. Shapard, Vice President and Cashier, the Bank of Halifax, Halifax: W. W. Early, Jr., President, The National Bank of Orange, Orange, and President, VBA; and H. Earl Cook, Chairman, FDIC
(From VBA Archives)

The legislative process waits on no man, and Virginia's banking community was surprised when a bill was introduced in both houses of the General Assembly on January 18, 1962, well before the VBA committee had an opportunity to recommend a position to the Convention scheduled in June.

The sponsors of the bill were presidents of two small banks, Fred Buck and Shirley T. Holland. Buck represented Abingdon in the House of Delegates; Holland of Isle of Wight was Chairman of the Senate Banking Committee. The Buck-Holland Committee bill, as amended, became law on July 1, 1962, and a new era for banking was to follow. For the first time since 1927 the Virginia Banking Act of 1962 provided for statewide expansion of Virginia banks, through merger. De novo branches still could not be established outside the area of each bank's charter location.

The branching laws were subsequently tinkered with from time to time, but did not see comprehensive change again until 1986 when all restrictions on branching were removed with the passage of a VBA-sponsored bill.

The history of branch banking in Virginia, as recited in an article published in *The Southern Banker,* September 1982, by Nicholas C. Kyrus, Deputy Commissioner, Virginia Bureau of Financial Institutions, said: "The Buck-Holland Amendment had a sweeping effect on Virginia banking structure. With the 1962 change in the branching laws, Virginia banks embarked on an unprecedented expansion, trying to catch up with ever-changing market conditions.

Kyrus pointed out that from 1962 to mid-1978, more than 200 holding company affiliations and mergers took place, transforming Virginia de facto into a statewide branching state.

"By the end of 1978 there were 1,302 branches in operation, up from 89 at the end of 1945, and 320 at the end of 1961," Kyrus said.

Another issue of paramount importance to Virginia bankers in the post-war years was interest rate ceilings on loans. The first break came in 1968 when the contract rate was raised from 6 percent to 8 percent and credit cards were authorized at a rate of 1.5 percent per month, or 18 percent a year. In the ensuing years, the Association continued to press its agenda for deregulated rates. Incrementally, rates were largely deregulated, the hardest fought battle occurring when the Association petitioned the Assembly in 1982 to remove the 18 percent lid on credit cards. The battle was contentious but successful.

Particularly with credit cards, the tug of war on rates and fees did not completely abate with the 1982 legislation. From time to time the VBA had to fight back proposals to reestablish the rate ceiling, or otherwise regulate credit cards. After fending off a serious legislative effort in 1982 to impose a free period mandate even when there was an unpaid balance, the credit card issue seemed to have, at long last, "matured" in 1992 when the Assembly responded positively to the industry's call to move towards a truly free market credit card by removing a statutory lid on late fees. VBA President Douglas D. Monroe, Jr., reporting to the membership, noted that key support was provided by Lieutenant Governor Don Beyer, who, he said, "went to the mat" for the deregulation bill.

Solving the interest rate problems did not solve tax problems. On at least two occasions, the industry had to provide solutions.

One of the solutions was the bank franchise tax enacted in 1980. This tax is in lieu of a previous bank shares tax, and is still in place today.

Another was a change in the law to provide that cash on hand in a bank would not continue to fall in the category of tax on capital not otherwise taxed. Prior to the adoption of the VBA bill, corporate cash accounts at banks would drastically shrink as year-end neared.

2

Aggressive Management and Marketing

"... bankers must realize that they are no longer the only kid on the block. There are new competitors. We must recognize these competitors and alter our long-standing practices to meet this challenge. But we must first admit there is a challenge. And I believe there is."
—VBA President Francis Bell, Jr. 1973 Convention

THE DECADE OF THE 1950S was a stable period in Virginia and the nation. But banking changes were becoming a reality. The Bank Holding Company Act of 1956 permitted the states to adopt holding company legislation. Virginia's own laws authorizing expansion by merger also had their impact. There was a rising tide of bank mergers, and as the years passed, it was obvious that financial institutions were becoming more geared to a mass market of consumers. Bank promotion touted the "full service" advantages of commercial banking.

The VBA underwent a realignment of the duties of its various committees in 1971. Banking was changing. The VBA adjusted to meet the challenge. Sales and marketing found meaning in an industry that had not previously bothered so much with such ideas.

The 1974 report of the VBA Committee on Public Relations and Marketing noted that "... the primary objective of this particular Committee has been concentrating and developing and increasing the marketing knowledge and skills of member banks, especially small and medium-sized banks."

Dr. Leonard L. Berry, Chairman of the Department of Marketing at Virginia Commonwealth University, was chosen as a special consultant. The economic education program developed by the VBA Committee with Dr. Berry's guidance was significant and caught the notice of the ABA. Dr. Berry was commissioned by the ABA to develop the program into a package for use by other state associations.

Banking had changed many times throughout history, and the tempo of change was increasing quickly.

As VBA President Francis Bell, Jr., a Harrisburg banker, had pointed out, bankers had to change the long-standing practices to meet the challenges.

Virginia bankers and their Association were doing just that. Banking had

The famous "Boat 'n Bank" of Chesapeake National Bank, Kilmarnock, operated from 1968 to 1977 as a floating bank that operated in three locations—on Carters Creek in Lancaster County, to help the watermen and their related interests. Says Doug Moore, Jr., Chairman and CEO, "the boat bank was a successful effort to take the cash to the watermen so that they wouldn't tie up our teller lines in our Irvington and Kilmarnock offices handling their lengthy cash transactions." Among the other unique features of the floating bank, according to Moore, "we were the only bank that was required to have its manager licensed boat captain."

changed many times throughout history, and the tempo of change was increasing quickly.

Had the founders of the VBA in 1893 been awakened from their slumber in the 1980s, they would have been befuddled by what had happened, much of it after World War II.

They would have found computers, automatic tellers, electronic funds transfers, a balance sheet with a strange construction of assets and liabilities, new forms of lending, credit cards and other innovations never dreamed of in 1893.

3

In Search of the "Level Playing Field"

"Stay With the Procession or You Will Never Catch Up."
—George Ade, Amercan humorist

JANUARY 1980 BROUGHT A NEW DECADE of dramatic changes in banking and finance.

The age of new technology already had a firm hold on the industry. Some of the old timers thought that the new crop of innovators in business and finance had suddenly started speaking in unknown tongues, using the language of computers as the tide of technology swept the banking shore.

The late 1960s and early 1970s foretold the pace of change that would usher in the 1980s. The ABA conducted a National Automation Survey in 1972 that showed automation was in full swing. Five percent of the smaller banks and 21.6 percent of the banks over $500 million already had cash dispensers and automated teller systems, the published results showed. The VBA and the bankers of the Commonwealth marched in the parade of technology. The age had started with many bankers concerned about the innovations, but they stuck with the new-fangled electronics.

As Mark Twain said, "All you need in this life is ignorance and confidence, and then success is sure." It must be remembered as a historical fact that Twain never saw a computer, and it is realistic to speculate that were he around today he might revise his humor to substitute "intelligence" for "ignorance" as he viewed in awe what technology has wrought.

Technology was not the only change that swept through the industry in the decade of the 1980s. Banking's permitted boundaries again bubbled to the top as major issues. The VBA was again called upon to take action. In 1983, the VBA Board instructed President Ralph Deacon to appoint a special Task Force on Interstate Banking. This he did with former VBA President Hovey Dabney serving as Chairman. The Task Force began work in 1983, but there was no consensus. There would be no interstate legislation in the 1984 General Assembly.

A couple of Southeastern states did put regional reciprocal interstate laws on the books in 1984. The VBA Task Force continued to function. Regional meetings were held with bank leaders around the state to gain broad input and develop a consensus. A special banker panel led a discussion on interstate banking at the Association's June Convention. Jack Jennings, then CEO of United Virginia Bank, and a proponent, observed that "after something had been done for 50 years someplace else, Virginia would adopt it as an experiment."

By late 1984, a consensus had emerged. Even many of those opposed to the idea came to share the view that Virginia could not be an island. The VBA would support a regional interstate approach. The issue, then, was pitched in the 1985 General Assembly and a statute was adopted.

The adoption of interstate banking was not the end of the debate on boundary restrictions. Later that same year, the Association began to debate whether the time had now come to adopt statewide branching. A consensus was developed. The answer was yes. The Association's statewide branching bill went to the 1986 Assembly and was adopted.

The Association's statewide branching bill went to the 1986 Assembly and a statute was adapted.

In his report to the 1986 VBA Convention, Executive Vice President Walter C. Ayers said, "I think it is interesting to note that in a span of barely twelve months, the General Assembly of Virginia enacted Regional Interstate Banking and Statewide Branch Banking, putting behind us in a matter of months geographical issues that have been the major source of dissension in the industry for years." Noting that the efforts made to bring the industry together on the two issues, Ayers observed that "there is strength in unity and weakness in division."

Despite all of the technological progress of the '80s, the movement to regional affiliations, and the adoption of statewide branching, all was not well in the banking industry. Banking was still searching for equity and "a level playing field." Nonbank competitors were making inroads, and banking's turf was threatened.

4

Competition a Reality—Deregulation

"I think we are driving the bankers up the wall."
—William Isaac, FDIC Chairman, 1982

RAMPANT INFLATION APPEARED IN THE LATE 1970S and the early 1980s. A large contingent of Virginia bankers were in New Orleans for the 1979 ABA Convention. Federal Reserve Chairman Paul Volcker was on the program. A capacity audience flocked to the hall to hear his address. News of the drastic action by the Fed to restrict monetary growth arrived simultaneously at the convention with Volcker.

At long last, many bankers believed the light at the end of the tunnel was visible. It was true—Volcker's light proved to be more than a flickering candle—the Federal Reserve had come to grips with the problem and pledged not to relent in its efforts.

Bankers had a full agenda: money market competition, NOW accounts, competition with other financial intermediaries, to list a few. But the overpowering issue was inflation and monetary control.

It was a time for action, and bankers were obliged to take a leading role. Money market funds, a fairly new phenomenon, appeared in financial circles a few years prior to 1980. By then, several billions of dollars had flowed from traditional intermediaries. Virginia bankers felt the impact. Interest rates soared, the prime rate reaching an all-time high in 1980 of 20.5 percent. The inflation rate climbed to more than 12 percent in 1980.

It was a time for action, and bankers were obliged to take a leading role.

What would bankers do? The first order of business was to preserve banking's market share and to cope with an array of unusual challenges.

The process of adjustment in regulations began in the years of the administration of President Jimmy Carter. On March 31, 1980, Carter signed the Financial Institutions Deregulation and Monetary Control Act (FIRA) to provide equality on interest rate ceilings for banks and thrifts on savings accounts linked to transaction accounts.

Virginia bankers had continued to keep in close contact with Congress to appeal for more equity in banking legislation. They also were ill at ease over the slow progress of the members of the DIDC (Depository Institutions Deregulation Committee) for the orderly phaseout of Regulation Q, as Congress had left this up to DIDC.

The big news came on March 22, 1982—DIDC announced the phaseout of Reg Q by May 1, 1982, with time ceilings eliminated on savings accounts having maturities of 3.5 years or more. Also announced was a new deposit instrument of a 91-day savings certificate with a minimum balance of $7,500, a change from the existing $10 thousand for the six-month money market certificate.

Bankers agreed that this was a positive step, for they felt that competition with the money market mutual funds, generally operated without regulations and ceilings, was unfair.

After a long summer, Congress passed the Garn-St Germain Depository Institutions Act of 1982 on September 30, 1982. President Ronald Reagan signed it into law on October 15.

DIDC was directed by Congress to announce final action on deregulation in 60 days. The action, effective January 1, 1984, established a new market rate account to compete with the money market mutual funds.

The real glamour part of the new law was the money market account, described as a "deregulatory splash" for commercial banks and other despository institutions.

Some probably thought that Christmas 1984 had come early! Others saw the rapid-changing world of finance as a stressful challenge. Said FDIC Chairman William Isaac, "I think we are driving bankers up the wall."

In his address to the 1986 Convention, VBA President Townsend Oast, a Chesapeake banker, evidenced the frustration alluded to by Isaac when he said, "We have stressed in various forums that the banking industry is not a deregulated industry, as is popularly perceived. We have emphasized that we have only deregulated the liability side and not the asset side of the ledger."

He urged persistence in the long-range effort to achieve "competitive equity in the marketplace by permitting banks to offer more product options."

At the 1987 VBA Convention the following year, VBA President Robert M.

Freeman, a Richmond banker, carried forward the theme. "I believe," he said, "that the future viability of the banking industry requires, even demands, that our legislators free us from the shackles that bind us in terms of our ability to compete in the marketplace."

VBA President H.B. Rew, who followed Freeman as Association President, continued to drive home the message in his report to the 1988 Convention. He noted that the Congress had moved backwards, adopting a moratorium on new bank powers. Rew announced that the Association was stepping up its efforts, and was now holding quarterly meetings with members of Congress.

In 1989, during the Presidential term of Sam Cardwell, the VBA took matters into its own hands, sponsoring a bill in the state legislature to permit banks to sell insurance. The battle raged through three successive legislative sessions, and the Presidential terms of John H. Clements and William F. Shumadine, Jr.

The VBA's competitive equity bill finally passed in 1991, and Virginia became the first state in recent history to grant such a blanket authorization to its banks. Noting the victory, President Shumadine, in his address to the 1991 Convention, referenced back to the words of Dizzy Dean, concluding that "it ain't bragging if you've done it; and by God, we've done it."

PART EIGHT

VBA's First Century—Banking Changes and Benchmarks of an Organization

1

Banking Legislation and Regulation—Consensus

"The success of each is dependent upon the success of the other."
—John D. Rockefeller, Jr.

SEEKING AND GETTING CONSENSUS for a trade association requires skill practically applied.

From the beginning of the VBA in 1893, the ever-changing banking environment has necessitated informed discussion and sincere application of fairness and integrity. Building a consensus within the industry on relevant issues has almost always been a precondition of getting anything of substance accomplished.

The consensus builder in Virginia has been the VBA. And what is the VBA? It is people—staff and bankers working together. Successive VBA managing officers, Marchant D. Wornom, Rawley F. Daniel, Marchant D. Wornom again, W.O. Pearce, and Walter C. Ayers, along with a skilled staff have played a vital role.

In the final analysis, however, consensus would not have been possible without team player banks and bankers. Perhaps more in Virginia than in most states, bankers have been team players. Association Presidents, officers, Board members, and indeed, rank and file bankers have frequently set aside their personal views or desires in the interest of compromise and achieving what is best for the whole. Evidence of this team spirit is strongly demonstrated by the fact that the VBA has enjoyed broad membership support. For several years now, every commercial bank headquartered in Virginia has chosen to be a VBA member—a claim few state associations can make.

This broad-based involvement of bank leaders in the Association and the consensus building it has made possible have yielded results.

At the 75th Annual Convention of the VBA, held June 19-22, 1968, President Thomas E. Sebrell, III, reviewed some of the highlights of the VBA. Said the Alexandria banker: "Leadership in finance, industrial development, agriculture, education, research—projected by men of integrity and vision—has brought action and accomplishment."

Of all the contributors, perhaps none are more notable than the high caliber and unselfish individuals who have led the Association as President. From the Association's first President, Walter H. Taylor of Norfolk, to current President Paul H. Geithner, Jr., of Falls Church—and incoming President Vernard W. Henley of Richmond—these leaders have been persons of success and character.

What are the VBA's most notable "footprints" in its first century? Many are recorded in this volume, none more important than the creation of the VBA—an organized association that has guided the bankers of the Old Dominion, insisting that programs and services be put in place to make a vast difference to banking and the public.

Speaking at the 1990 VBA Convention, Executive Vice President Walter C. Ayers said, "A trade association has as its mission the accomplishment of objectives that individual members of that association would find difficult or impossible to accomplish if they had to act individually. Almost universally, these objectives fall into one of three broad categories: governmental relations, information and education and the provision of economic services or benefits."

The VBA continues to perform these functions through its inordinately high quality of volunteer leadership and staff.

2

Bankers in the Classroom—Educational Emphasis

"Ours in the best."
—From the report by Jesse Wood, Richmond banker, on the first VBA Bankers Conference at the Univeristy of Virginia in 1938

ARISTOTLE IS QUOTED AS SAYING that education was "an adornment in prosperity and a refuge in adversity."

The economic doldrums of the 1930s had tested the mettle of banking and Virginia bankers. They responded in many ways, not the least of which was to better train themselves.

Fifty-five years ago—in August 1938—the first Virginia Bankers Conference was held at the University of Virginia in Charlottesville.

It would become a major factor in banking education. VBA President Alexander F. Ryland, a Richmond banker, turned to Jesse F. Wood, also a Richmond banker, to serve as chairman of the VBA Banking Education and Public Relations Committee.

At the VBA Convention in Hot Springs, Wood was recognized to promote the first session of the Conference. He confidently told his audience that the gathering should appeal to "every banker in Virginia who doesn't know all the answers to banking questions." Beginning with the 1952 session, the name was changed to the Virginia Bankers School.

By the late 1950s, it was apparent that the banking environment had again substantially changed, and that a new, more comprehensive approach to education was needed. Eddie Wayne, Executive Vice President of the Federal Reserve Bank of Richmond, was tapped by the Association as a consultant to recommend an approach to the Trustees headed by Robert H. Daniel.

Mr. Wayne subsequently recommended, and the VBA concurred, that a more intensive management level school was needed. In 1959, the first session of the Virginia Bankers School under a new, more intensive three-year format convened at the University of Virginia. The first class of the reorganized school graduated in 1961.

The highly successful school, now known as the Virginia Bankers School of Bank Management, continues today. Jesse Wood's opinion in 1938 that "ours is the best" is still valid today.

No doubt that it took a lot of confidence to start an educational program at a time when Virginia and the nation were emerging from the Great Depression.

VBA members continue to respond to the leadership challenge. In addition to numerous educational seminars, the Association has created two new schools— a Compliance School and a Lending to Small Business School. Both have met with wide acceptance.

3

Banking Chains—Prominence Recognized

"Next to my own family, the Federal Reserve System is nearest to my heart."
—Virginia Congressman Carter Glass

THE ROLE PLAYED BY MANY PROMINENT VIRGINIANS in the history of banking has been noted throughout this history. To what have been specifically recognized by the Virginia Bankers Association and its member banks deserves special note.

In 1968, the VBA launched a fundraising campaign to fund two chairs at the University of Virginia. The money was raised and the Carter Glass Chair was established in 1969, followed by the A. Willis Robertson Chair in 1970. In fact, the fundraising effort, supported nationally by the ABA, was so successful, a third chair, the Virginia Bankers Association Chair of Bank Management was also established.

The Glass and Robertson chairs were established in the Department of Economics and the Bank Management Chair in the McIntire School of Commerce.

A Willis Robertson served first in the U.S. House of Representatives, and then in the U.S. Senate where he became the Chairman of the Senate Banking and Currency Committee. Robertson is generally given much of the credit for the passage of the Bank Holding Company Act of 1956, and other banking legislation of that period.

Carter Glass is credited by many as being one of the chief architects of the Act creating the Federal Reserve System. His name is permanently associated with the legislation that limits the affiliation between securities and lending firms - the Glass-Stegall Act. Glass was also a key player in the debate that led to the creation of the Federal Deposit Insurance Corporation in 1933.

4

Young Bankers Section

"... a Young Bankers Section of the VBA could make untold contributions to the Senior Association and the banking industry of Virginia."
—J.A. Wilson, Jr., Chairman YBS Steering Committee

On September 10, 1969, a special steering committee met at the VBA Office to consider the feasibility of making a recommendation to the VBA Board on the establishment of a Young Bankers Section. The Steering Committee was chaired by Jerry A. Wilson, Jr., a Blackstone banker, and included other bankers such as Lindsay B. Clarke, Warner N. Dalhouse, Robert L. High, L. David Horner, III, W.R. Hudson, Earl R. Johnston, Randolph W. McElroy, Jesse B. Shearin, Jr., Harry H. Warner, C. Lee Wilkinson, Bruce R. Hazelgrove, and VBA Staff members Marchant D. Wornom and Edward D. Seidel.

The VBA Board approved the organization of the Young Bankers Section at its 1970 Convention, and the Bylaws of the Section were subsequently printed. On October 30, 1970, a special YBS Nominating Committee was convened, and the following slate of officers assumed leadership roles of the Section: President - L. David Horner, III; First Vice President - Warner N. Dalhouse; and Second Vice President - C. Lee Wilkinson, Jr. The first six group Executive Committeemen were as follows: George Yowell - Group I; Gari Sullivan - Group II; Doug Kyle - Group III; Rodger Fauber - Group IV; Worth Carter - Group V; and Jesse Shearin - Group VI. This slate of officers was ratified at the first annual YBS Conference held at the Sheraton-Fredericksburg Motor Inn, October 28-29, 1970.

That the subsequent accomplishments of this group have been phenomenal should come as no surprise when one takes into account the names of those who assumed leadership roles in the newly formed organization. The leadership qualities exhibited by these people were later recognized by their own institutions as many of them went on to become CEOs or to occupy other senior level positions.

From its initial launching right through to today, the VBA's Young Bankers Section has had a strong, enviable record of accomplishments. The group has always been committed to the economic education of Virginia's school children. In fact, Virginia was one of the pilot states asked by the American Bankers Association to become involved in the PEP Program (Personal Economics Program) in 1979, due in large part to the success the Virginia group had had with its own Project REBS (Regional Educational Banker Services), which the group started in 1971.

Hardly a year has passed that the Virginia YBS has not attained major recognition and awards at the ABA's Annual PEP States Meeting. In fact, any one of Virginia's six groups reaches more individuals and does more presentations than many states that are involved in the PEP Program. That is truly some accomplishment.

The group has gradually expanded its base over the years, and its programs now include an annual Bank Day for high school seniors, as well as legislative support and award-winning public relations and marketing efforts.

This is all due in large part to the foresight of Jerry A. Wilson and the initial group of Virginia bankers on the steering committee that saw a need for Virginia's young bankers to become involved in the efforts of their Association and to take an interest in the future of their industry.

5

Taking Care of Bank Employees

THE VIRGINIA BANKERS ASSOCIATION CAME EARLY to the concept that one of its functions should be to assist its member banks in providing needed benefits to employees. Starting at least as early as the 1940s, the VBA put into place its first group health plan. Over the years, the program has evolved in a major sort of way, both in terms of the coverages provided, and its administration.

Today, participating banks can cover their employees with a range of benefits including major medical, dental, life, disability, thrift and 401Ks, pension, deferred compensation, and split dollar life. Not only can banks choose among product options, but also delivery options, including a flex plan that allows employee selection.

Another innovation has been the creation of a separate corporation to administer the program. This approach has enabled the complete separation of the benefits program from the dues-based VBA budget. The program, then, has become completely self-funded.

The Benefits Corporation Board of Directors consists of President Robert H. Gilliam, Jr., and members G. William Beale, John H. Clements, Hugh W. Compton, Larry G. Dillon, Marshall H. Groom, William H. Hayter, V.W. Henley, Homer L. Hite, James M. Ratliff, Robert F. Shuford and Donald R. Yowell.

6

A Legend in His Own Time

PERHAPS NO INDIVIDUAL IN THE HISTORY OF VIRGNIA BANKING has more firmly affixed his imprint on the state's banking industry than Jack Edmonds, III. Edmonds was outside legal counsel for the Association for 27 years, 1964 to 1991.

In his 27-year tenure, hardly a change was made in the code affecting banking that did not first have his input, even when the Association had no position. Many were the times that Edmonds would be summoned from his seat by a Committee Chairman or member to "explain" some provision of banking law that was the subject of a bill under consideration. One senior member of the Corporation, Insurance and Banking Committee was often heard summoning Edmonds to the podium with the words "where is my lawyer—get my lawyer up here to explain this thing." Needless to say, having an Association lawyer who enjoyed that kind of respect from legislators enured to the benefit of Virginia's banking industry.

The VBA honored Edmonds at its 1992 Convention. In his remarks, President Douglas D. Monroe, Jr., observed that "the lesser informed referred to Virginia's banking laws as the 'Code of Virginia'; whereas those who had been close to the process of law making over the last 27 years, and really knew the extent of Jack Edmonds' influence on that process, referred to our banking laws as the 'Code of Edmonds'."

7

Lois Lee Remembers

ON FRIDAY, JUNE 13, 1975, delegates and guests were at The Homestead in Hot Springs for a very special reason—the Retirement Party of VBA Secretary Lois R. Lee to honor her for "Thirty years of dedicated service."

Lois, a North Carolina native, who liked Virginia, arrived in Richmond in 1934 and taught penmanship and accounting in business school until 1940. From 1940-1942, she taught in the business department of the Louisa County School business department. In the summer of 1942 she was employed by the U.S. Employment Service in Richmond, and worked with the U.S. Army Finance Office in Richmond until the end of World War II in 1945.

Her career with the VBA began in November 1945 when Thomas D. Neal was Secretary. She remembers her first VBA convention in 1946 at Virginia Beach when P.W. Anderson was VBA President.

In the summer of 1954 she took vacation time to visit banks in Southwestern Virginia. In one week she visited 20 banks.

The VBA presented Lois four volumes of letters from bank officers. Here are a few of the quotes:

S. Ray Carter, the National Bank of Chilhowie, wrote, "I recall a few years back you used your vacation time to visit us bankers way down here in Southwest Virginia ...."

From F. Carbery Ritchie, The National Bank of Fairfax: "... I am greatly disturbed. Who is going to run VBA? We all know you nursed it, changed its diapers, Rawley's and Marchant's too, all these many years."

There was no end to the good wishes for Lois R. Lee, and she proudly recalls her pleasant 30 years at the VBA. She and her sister are retired and live at the family home and farm near Four Oaks and Benson in her native North Carolina community. But Lois never pulled up her roots in Virginia!

8

Wornom-to-Daniel-to-Wornom

THE VBA CONVENTION AT THE HOMESTEAD, JUNE 14-16, 1962, marked significant milestones in the Association's professional management.

Executive Vice President Rawley F. Daniel resigned in February to enter commercial banking. He had served for 10 years (June 1952-February 1962).

Marchant D. Wornom, who was managing officer from 1946 to 1952, when he resigned to become an official of a private college, returned to the VBA post to succeed Daniel. He told the convention that he was happy to be back with the VBA after a ten-year "sabbatical."

VBA President H. Ewing Wall told the convention: "Rawley has rendered invaluable and outstanding service to the Association during the past ten years, and we were greatly distressed at his leaving." He told of a testimonial dinner in Richmond held in Rawley's honor.

"Your officers" he said "were charged with the responsibility of finding a suitable replacement ... who could come into the office and take over with a minimum of interruption in the program .... We are indeed happy to have Marchant D. Wornom, our former Executive Vice President, back with us in the position vacated by Rawley Daniel."

Resolutions were adopted that recognized the many and important contributions of EVP Daniel and expression of pleasure at the return of EVP Wornom.

Maggie Walker: "Let us have a bank that will take the nickels and turn them into dollars."

9

Maggie Walker—Precedent Setter

"Let us have a bank that will take the nickles and turn them into dollars."

RICHMOND'S MAGGIE L. WALKER WAS AN INNOVATOR, a precedent setter, and she had the force of intellect and leadership when she spoke these words to a meeting of the councils of the Independent Order of Saint Luke, a black fraternal insurance organization in Richmond in August 1901.

As a result of her inspirational words, according to the report of the event, a resolution was quickly adopted to create the Saint Luke Penny Savings Bank.

The bank was chartered and opened its doors located at 902-904 St. James Street on November 2, 1903, under the newly adopted corporation laws of Virginia.

Maggie Walker was elected its first president, becoming the "first woman bank president in the United States." She had announced a goal of $25,000 for the first day's deposits. "This amount had nearly been reached today (Monday, November 2, 1903) at 2 o'clock," the *News Leader* reported.

The black bank, according to reports, had President Walker, Cashier Emmett C. Burke, and nine clerks. This bank was the predecessor by merger in 1930 of the Consolidated Bank and Trust Company.

Maggie Walker died in 1934. At the time she was chairman of Consolidated's board.

The bank's current chairman is Vernard W. Henley, incoming President of the VBA.

10

VBA Recognized for Preservation

THE AMERICAN BANKERS ASSOCIATION was 100 years old in 1975. As a leading part of that observance, the spotlight was put on 200 years of American banking, and bank and state bankers association projects competed for recognition.

The Virginia Bankers Association, over a three-year period, has contributed $6,000 towards the restoration of one of the oldest known bank buildings in the U.S.

The circa-1800 building was the Petersburg branch of the Farmers Bank of Virginia from 1817 until it closed in 1867—a casualty of the Civil War.

The building was acquired and restored by the Association of Virginia Antiquities, which now maintains a museum open to the public on the first floor. Both associations feel the restored building is a most suitable testimonial to the important role banking played in the rapid growth of American industry, commerce and transportation systems in the first half of the 19th century.

(From: ABA, 200 Years of American Banking, 1975.)

The association's top recognition was won by the Virginia Bankers Association.

The ABA booklet said: "The Virginia Bankers Association, over a three-year period, has contributed $6,000 towards the restoration of one of the oldest known bank buildings in the U.S.

"The circa-1800 building was the Petersburg branch of the Farmers Bank of Virginia from 1817 until it closed in 1867—a casualty of the Civil War.

"The building was acquired and restored by the Association of Virginia Antiquities which now maintains a museum open to the public on the first floor. Both associations feel the restored building is a most suitable testimonial to the important role banking played in the rapid growth of America for preservation of industry, commerce and transportation systems in the first half of the 19th century."

11

State Bank Supervision

THE STATE CORPORATION COMMISSION WAS CREATED by the Virginia Constitution of 1902. Regulation of banking was given to the Commission in 1910. Since that time the banking laws of Virginia have been administered through many officers with various titles.

The title of Commissioner of Banking was observed from 1938 to June 30, 1978. Sidney A. Bailey served in that office from June 1, 1977 to June 30, 1978, when his title was changed effective July 1, 1978, to Commissioner of Financial Institutions. He has served in that capacity to date.

The 1922 13th Annual Report of the Banking Division reported the following: "The 1922 General Assembly enacted what is generally known as a 'Credit Union Law.' So far only one credit union has been authorized by the State Corporation Commission to do business, being the one operated at the Hampton Institute. It therefore remains to be seen whether or not this legislation will be useful to the citizens of Virginia."

12

Nostalgia, Traditions—The World of Banking

"In Virginia"

IN GRANDILOQUENT STYLE, the bankers at the VBA Conventions of earlier years heard long and flowery speeches. Take the 1904 convention at Old Point Comfort. In his address of welcome, Honorable Mayrus Jones of Newport News said in part: "You have gathered upon the banks of the most historic waters in the New World. When the King of Day first emerges from his eastern gates he illumines the waters here—those which were the first to be plied by Anglo–Saxon ships on this continent .... Upon the banks of this noble river the cradle of a great nation was rocked .... No man need ever be ashamed to be called a Virginian, for her name shall be linked with that of Athens and Rome, and will go down through the ages as the brightest gem that graces the crown of this nation."

VBA President Henry L. Schmelz of Hampton recognized E.S. Reid, Chatham banker, to give the response. After the usual opening remarks, he said: "I am afraid some enterprising city, it its efforts to outstrip its neighbors, will propose before long a balloon ascension, or a trip in an airship, but as we have all seen enough of the inflation and air bubbles which have been so fashionable lately in the industrial world, I think, as conservative Virginia bankers, it is a good time to keep on terra firma, or a least, close to shore .... It is a great pleasure to us who live far in the interior, where a creek looks as big as a river and a river as big as an ocean, to come down to see these mighty waters ...."

Reid read the famous poem, "In Virginia," used for many years in the printed convention *Proceedings:*

"The roses bloom nowhere so white,
As in Virginia
The sunshine nowhere shines so bright,
As in Virginia
The birds sing nowhere quite so sweet
And nowhere hearts so lightly beat,
For heaven and earth doth seem to meet
In Old Virginia.

The days are never quite so long,
As in Virginia;
Nor quite so filled with happy song
As in Virginia
And when my time has come to die,
Just take me back and let me lie

Close where the James goes rolling by
In Old Virginia.

There is nowhere a land so fair
As Old Virginia. So full of song, so free of care,
As Old Virginia.
And I believe that happy land
The Lord prepared for mortal man
Is built exactly on the plan
Of Old Virginia."

*

The 1907 Convention was held at the Jamestown Exposition, with A.B. Schwarzkopf of Norfolk as VBA President.

*

The first off-shore VBA Convention was held in 1939—a cruise to Bermuda. Clarence L. Robey of Purcellville was VBA President.

*

Two father-son combinations have served as President of the VBA: Giles H. Miller, Lynchburg, 1939-1940, and Giles H. Miller, Jr., Culpeper, 1950-1951; Shirley T. Holland, Windsor, 1957-1958, and Richard J. Holland, Windsor, 1973- 1974.

*

Published hotel rates for the 1917 VBA Convention at the Hotel Chamberlin, Old Point Comfort, convention headquarters, were:

Single room, one person per day	$5.00
Double room, two persons	9.00
Single room, with bath, one person	6.00
Double room, with bath, two persons	10.00

The prices included all meals.

*

"Preacher" Paschal B. Knight, National Bank Examiner, in the Dallas region of Texas, retired in 1979. He was asked to write his colorful memoirs. He did. Called "Memwas," Knight sat down at his old typewriter, called "Old Blessed," and recalled many of his experiences. From 1947 to 1979 he wore out 17 automobiles. His beginning annual salary was $2,924.96, with $6 per diem. "Preacher had a case to carry "Old Blessed" in, and written on it was:

BLESSED IS HE WHO HAS COLLATERAL FOR HE SHALL BE PAID.

Here are a few of the one-liners Knight put in his booklet:

Two things I don't want to miss—a free meal and a bad loan.

Every day is judgement day. Use some today.

Borrowing money is like drinking whiskey—both are good if you don't overdo it.

Sometimes it takes a lot of scratching around to get you out of a deal you were itching to get into.

When you are feeling "Tolible" it means you feel well enough to eat but you don't feel like working.

Taking the easy path is what makes rivers and people crooked.

Preacher said some of the banks he examined in the early years of his career were so small that it was said of him that he could drive up, leave his car's engine running, examine the bank, get back in his car and be on his way in a few minutes.

*

Carter Glass and his two-minute speech are legendary in banking circles. In 1935 Glass was in the U.S. Senate from Virginia. The venerable godfather of many banking acts, including the Federal Reserve, was a political conservative, and he began to have some serious doubts about the New Deal of President Franklin D. Roosevelt. It was not unusual for him to kick out of the traces of the Democratic Party and its smiling leader in the White House.

Speaking to the graduating class of Tufts College in June 1935, he said, "A *new deal* relates itself somehow to playing cards. Cards, as you very well know, are largely used for gambling purposes. So, when you have a *new deal,* you should make certain too many cards are not passed to the players on one side of the table and too few to those on the other side." Period. End of graduating address. It is said that his entire remarks took only two minutes.

*

Things have changed a lot since 1944. The Department of Labor that year announced a wage scale of 40 cents an hour for bank employees.

Hurrah for a living wage!

*

From the Civil War to early 1935, national banks issued their notes. The Treasury called in all Panama Canal Bonds and Consols for redemption on July 1, 1935. It was goodbye to bank notes and circulation privileges which national banks prized for 70 years.

*

At the 1962 VBA Convention, presided over by H. Ewing Wall of Quantico, a speaker read a poem written by a college youth, G.L. Huemminger, first published in the *Penn State Froth,* November 1915:

> "Tobacco is a dirty word. I like it.
> It satisfies no normal need. I like it.
> It makes you thin, it makes you lean,
> It takes the hair right off your bean.
> It's the worst darn stuff I've ever seen.
> I like it."

*

In the June 26, 1972 issue of the Norfolk *Virginian-Pilot,* a column by George H. Tucker gives another dimension to the venerated first president of the VBA, Colonel Walter Herron Taylor.

"Taylor was a bon vivant, and his home was famous for its good living, one of his specialties being his punch, celebrated throughout the length and breadth of the Old Dominion," Tucker wrote.

"The recipe was labeled 'Fish House Punch.' Just one reading of it and you are tipsy," the columnist wrote.

Here is Colonel Taylor's "Fish House Punch" recipe:

"Make a syrup of three Quarts of Water, one Pound of Brown Sugar, pour it over the rinds and juice of a Dozen or a Dozen and a half Lemons. Cool. Add two quarts of Jamaica Rum, one quart of Brandy, dash well with Peach Brandy to make it mellow and extra fine. Serve in a bowl of crushed ice. To serve immediately, add one Quart of Pineapple juice instead of three Quarts of Water."

In giving a friend a copy of the recipe, Mrs. Taylor "hoisted this warning signal: 'Walter says look out for a swelled head the next morning,'" Tucker wrote.

*

In December 1863, Hugh McCulloch, Comptroller of the Currency, addressed a letter to all national banks under his jurisdiction.

Here are some of his paragraphs:

"Let no loans be made that are not secured beyond a reasonable contingency. Do nothing to foster and encourage speculation. Give facilities only to legitimate and prudent transactions ....

"Distribute your loans rather than concentrate them in a few hands. Large loans to a single individual or firm, although sometimes proper and necessary, are generally injudicious, and frequently unsafe ....

"Treat your customers liberally, bearing in mind the fact that a bank prospers as its customers prosper, but never permit them to dictate your policy.

"Pay your officials such salaries as will enable them to live comfortably and respectably without stealing; and require of them their entire services. If an officer lives beyond his income, dismiss him; even if his excess of expenditures can be explained consistently with his integrity, still dismiss him. Extravagance, if not a crime, very naturally leads to crime. A man cannot be a safe officer of a bank who spends more than he earns.

"A man cannot be a safe officer of a bank who spends more than he earns."

"The capital of a bank should be a reality, not a fiction; and it should be owned by those who have money to lend, and not to borrowers ....

"Pursue a straightforward, upright, legitimate banking business. Never be tempted by the prospect of large returns to do anything but what may be properly done under the National Currency Act. 'Splendid financiering' is not legitimate banking, and 'splendid financiers' in banking are generally either humbugs or rascals."

PART NINE

For the Record

1

VBA Records in the Flood

BACK IN 1938, Miss Lillian A. Kendall, VBA Assistant Secretary, attempted to round up some of the missing early records of the Association. She wrote to Secretary C.W. Beerbower, a Roanoke banker. He responded that he had found yearbooks from 1903 to 1937, inclusive, and six duplicates. He also listed many other later records. Secretary Beerbower wrote that his predecessor, W.S. Irby, had reported his files incomplete.

Beerbower concluded with this explanation to Miss Kendall: "It is a fact that a part of these records were stored in a basement vault that was completely submerged for 24 hours, during a flood here [Roanoke] several years ago; practically all the bank books, correspondence, etc. prior to that date were a hopeless wreck and were hauled out and burned ... this is most unfortunate, but it is due to what the law would say I think 'An Act of God.'"

2

Ten Banks Pre-Date VBA

THE VBA WAS FORMED IN 1893. To know that banking has changed, one need only look at the fact that just 10 banks pre-date the VBA in terms of still existing as they were chartered.

Burke & Herbert Bank & Trust, Alexandria	1852
National Bank of Fredericksburg	1865
Citizens Bank & Trust Company, Blackstone	1873
The Bank of Marion	1874
Bank of Fincastle	1875
Bank of Clarke County, Berryville	1881
Powell Valley National Bank, Jonesville	1888
Bank of Tazewell County, Tazewell	1889
National Bank of Blacksburg	1891
Page Valley National Bank, Luray	1893

3

VBA Group System Began in 1908

In 1907 the VBA Executive Committee recommended that the matter of dividing the state into groups "be referred to the 1908 Convention for consideration and adoption."

At the 1908 Convention at Hot Springs the Executive Committee recommended, and the members adopted, a proposal for the state to be divided into five groups. In 1922 a sixth group was added to the VBA configuration.

Due to consolidations and speed of transportation the Visa Groups were disbanded in 1992.

4

VBA Presidents, Dates and Convention Places

PAST PRESIDENTS OF THE VIRGINIA BANKERS ASSOCIATION

1894-95	*Walter H. Taylor, Norfolk	Norfolk
1895-96	*H.S. Trout, Roanoke	Norfolk
1896-97	*Caldwell Hardy, Norfolk	Old Point Confort
1897-98	*R.W. Burke, Staunton	Richmond
1898-99	*William M. Hill, Richmond	Richmond
1899-1900	*Mann S. Quarles, Richmond	Richmond
1900-01	*C.D. Fishburne, Charlottesville	Roanoke
1901-02	*George J. Seay, Richmond	Savannah, Ga.
1902-03	*Oliver J. Sands, Richmond	Lynchburg
1903-04	*Henry L. Schmelz, Hampton	Old Point Comfort
1904-05	*William M. Habliston, Richmond	Richmond
1905-06	*S.N. Hansborough, Winchester	Old Point Comfort
1906-07	*A.B. Schwarzkopf, Norfolk	Jamestown Exposition
1907-08	*Richard H. Smith, Richmond	Hot Springs
1908-09	*Joseph Stebbins, South Boston	Old Point Comfort
1909-10	*Henry A. Walker, Staunton	Old Point Comfort
1910-11	*J. William Miller, Pulaski	Hot Springs
1911-12	*Edgar P. Miller, Lynchburg	Old Point Comfort
1912-13	*Thomas B. McAdams, Richmond	Old Point Comfort
1913-14	*Joseph M. Hurt, Blackstone	Old Point Comfort
1914-15	*W.B. Vest, Newport News	Old Point Comfort
1915-16	*C.E. Tiffany, Warrenton	Old Point Comfort
1916-17	*E.B. Spencer, Roanoke	Old Point Comfort
1917-18	*W.M. Addison, Richmond	Old Point Comfort
1918-19	*G.E. Vaughan, Lynchburg	Old Point Comfort
1919-20	*R.G. Vance, Waynesboro	Hot Springs
1920-21	*T.F. Tilghman, Norfolk	Hot Springs
1921-22	*N.H. Williams, Chase City	Hot Springs
1922-23	*G.R. Ratcliffe, Manassas	Richmond
1923-24	*E.W. Tinsley, Roanoke	Norfolk
1924-25	*J.J. Scott, Bedford	Hot Springs
1925-26	*Walker Scott, Richmond	Roanoke
1926-27	*M.G. Field, Orange	Virginia Beach
1927-28	*J. Marshall Lewis, Gloucester	Old Point Comfort

1928-29	*E.S. Shields, Farmville	Old Point Comfort
1929-30	*C.S. Carter, Bristol	Hot Springs
1930-31	*C.C. Barksdale, Richmond	Old Point Comfort
1931-32	*W. Scott Irby, Kenbridge	Old Point Comfort
1932-33	*S.W. Keys, Glade Spring	Hot Springs
1933-34	*S.H. Plummer, Newport News	Virginia Beach
1934-35	*Carroll Pierce, Alexandria	Hot Springs
1935-36	*J. Sinclair Brown, Salem	Virginia Beach
1936-37	*James B. Dey, Jr., Norfolk+	
1936-37	*Milton R. Morgan, Eagle Rock	White Sulphur Springs
1937-38	*Alexander F. Ryland, Richmond	Hot Springs
1938-39	*Clarence L. Robey, Purcellville	Cruise—Bermuda
1939-40	*Giles H. Miller, Lynchburg	Roanokc
1940-41	*Thomas H. Blanton, Bowling Green	Richmond
1941-42	*G. Franklin Lenz, Newport News	Roanoke
1942-43	*G.C. McCall, Norton	Richmond
1943-44	*W.A. Roper, Richmond	Roanoke
1944-45	*C.T. O'Neill, Charlottesville	None held
1945-46	*P.W. Anderson, Marshall	Virginia Beach
1946-47	*Joseph E. Healy, Hampton	Virginia Beach
1947-48	*Warren M. Goddard, Richmond	Hot Springs
1948-49	*C. Francis Cocke, Richmond	Hot Springs
1949-50	*John S. Alfriend, Norfolk	Hot Springs
1950-51	Giles H. Miller, Jr. Culpeper	Hot Springs
1951-52	*R.F. Burke Steele, Petersburg	Roanoke
1952-53	*W.M. Early, Jr., Orange	Hot Springs
1953-54	*A.E. Anderson, Bristol	Cruise—Nassau, Havana
1954-55	*W.W. Shapard, Halifax	Hot Springs
1955-56	*H.H. Cooley, Round Hill	Hot Springs
1956-57	*Charles A. Kramer, Fredericksburg	Hot Springs
1957-58	*Shirley T. Holland, Windsor	Hot Springs
1958-59	*Robert T. Marsh, Jr., Richmond	Hot Springs
1959-60	*H.V. Lindsey, Richlands	Hot Springs
1960-61	Robert C. deRosset, Lynchburg	Hot Springs
1961-62	*H. Ewing Wall, Quantico	Hot Springs
1962-63	W.T. Robinson, West Point	Hot Springs
1963-64	*R.A. Duncan, Williamsburg	Cruise—Bermuda
1964-65	James W. Rawles, Richmond	Hot Springs
1965-66	*S.S. Flythe, Martinsville	Hot Springs
1966-67	*Brantley F. Barr, Danville	Hot Springs
1967-68	Thomas E. Sebrell, III, Alexandria	Hot Springs
1968-69	*Paul O. Hirschbiel, Staunton	Hot Springs
1969-70	James R. Austin, Orange	Cruise—San Juan, St. Thomas
1970-71	*John W. Boyle, Roanoke	Hot Springs
1971-72	Hovey S. Dabney, Charlottesville	Hot Springs
1972-73	Francis Bell, Jr., Harrisonburg	Hot Springs
1973-74	Richard J. Holland, Windsor	Hot Springs
1974-75	*Herbert C. Moseley, Richmond	Hot Springs
1975-76	*Ralph A. Beeton, Falls Church	Hot Springs
1976-77	C. Clarke Cunningham, Jr., Radford	Cruise—Bermuda
1977-78	*William H. Jefferson, Jr., Danville	Hot Springs
1978-79	George P. Beard, Jr., Culpeper	Hot Springs
1979-80	John B. Bernhardt, Norfolk	Hot Springs
1980-81	C. Coleman McGehee, Richmond	Hot Springs
1981-82	Milton L. Drewer, Jr., McLean	White Sulphur Springs
1982-83	*William T. Clements, Norton	Hot Springs
1983-84	Ralph L. Deacon, Charlottesville	Hot Springs
1984-85	John W. Lainhart, III, Warrenton	Hot Springs
1985-86	Townsend Oast, Chesapeake	Hot Springs
1986-87	Robert M. Freeman, Richmond	Hot Springs
1987-88	H.B. Rew, Jr., Onley	Hot Springs
1988-89	Samuel P. Cardwell, Richmond	Hot Springs
1989-90	John H. Clements, Carson	Hot Springs
1990-91	William F. Shumadine, Jr., Richmond	White Sulphur Springs
1991-92	Douglas D. Monroe, Jr., Kilmarnock	Hot Springs
1992-93	Paul H. Geithner, Jr., Falls Church	Hot Springs

*deceased

5

List of Past Executive Vice Presidents, Secretaries, Treasurers, and Past Attorneys

Walter C. Ayers

Walter C. Ayers has been Executive Vice President of the Virginia Bankers Association since October, 1983.

Before joining the VBA, Walter was Executive Director of the Virginia Petroleum Council, having previously served in staff positions at the Virginia Farm Bureau and the Virginia State Chamber of Commerce.

Walter is active in the community, having served as chairman of the Board of Deacons of Derbyshire Baptist Church, as a board member of his civic club, and is currently serving on the Board of Trustees of The Steward School. He has also been active in statewide endeavors, having been a Gubernatorial appointee to the Virginia Coal and Energy Study Commission and the Commission to study the Shortage of Family Physicians. He has also served on the Board of the Virginia Society of Association Executives.

Walter's role as Executive Vice President of the VBA has reached beyond Virginia. He served on the American Bankers Association Deposit Insurance Task Force that recommended some of the reforms made by Congress in deposit insurance in 1992. Walter was elected by his peers to serve the 1992-93 term as Chairman of the State Association Division of the ABA. He also served as Chairman of the Graduate School of Banking of the South in 1992-93.

A native of Patrick County, Virginia, Walter is a graduate of Ferrum Junior College and the College of William and Mary. He is married to the former Evelyn Lynn Parker of Wachapreague. Walter and Lynn have two sons.

Marchant D. Wornom

Rawley F. Daniel

W. O. Pearce

PAST MANAGING OFFICERS OF THE VBA

PAST SECRETARIES

*Samuel G. Wallace, Richmond
*Henry A. Williams, Richmond
*Norborn P. Gatling, Lynchburg
*V. Vaiden, Farmville
*Wallace Scott, Richmond
*W. F. Augustine, Richmond
*W. S. Irby, Kenbridge
*C. W. Beerbower, Roanoke
**John H. Payne, Richmond
***Thomas D. Neal, Richmond
Rawley F. Daniel, Richmond
Lois R. Lee

PAST ASSISTANT SECRETARIES

*Harry Frazier, Jr., Richmond
*Lillian Kendall, Richmond
*Elizabeth Keys Lammie, Richmond

PAST TREASURERS

*Samuel G. Wallace, Richmond
*Henry A. Williams, Richmond
*Julien H. Hill, Richmond
*W. F. Augustine, Richmond
*F. D. Maphis, Strasburg
*W. S. Irby, Kenbridge
*C. W. Beerbower, Roanoke
*Thomas D. Neal, Richmond
John H. Payne, Richmond

PAST ATTORNEYS

*George Bryan, Richmond
*Thomas O. Ozlin, Kenbridge
*J. Randolph Tucker, Richmond
*David J. Mays, Richmond
J. Randolph Tucker, Jr., Richmond
John W. Edmonds, III, Richmond

*deceased
**First full time managing officer in 1941
***Second full time managing officer

6

VBA Staff

Left to right, Barbara A. Garrett, Norman K. Robinson, Walter C. Ayers, and Bruce T. Whitehurst. All are Vice Presidents, except Ayers who is Executive Vice President.

Seated, Left to right, Norman K. Robinson, Bruce T. Whitehurst, Barbara A. Garrett and Walter C. Ayers. Standing, left to right, John B. Vellines, Susan D. Mason, Bette J. Albert, Pamela E. Parker, Deborah Happel, Robert Poole, Lois B. Blow, Gail N. Askew, Jennifer Scott, Glenda C. Cochran, and J. L. Roy Allison, Jr.

7

ABA Presidents from Virginia

VIRGINIA BANKING HAS FURNISHED three president of the American Bankers Association. The first was Caldwell Hardy of Norfolk in 1902. Thomas B. McAdams of Richmond, headed the ABA in 1921, and C. Francis Cocke of Roanoke was president in 1951. Each had served as VBA president prior to their service in the top leadership post.

8

Virginia Banks and Their CEOs

American National Bank & Trust Co., Danville-James A. Motley, Chairman and CEO
Bank First, NA, McLean-Thomas E. Williams, President and CEO
Bank of Alexandria, Alexandria-J. David Holden, President
Bank of Buchanan, Buchanan-H. Watts Steger, III, President and CEO
Bank of Carroll, Hillsville-J. David Cothran, President and CEO
Bank of Charlotte County, Phenix-Bobby A. Howard, President
Bank of Clarke County, Berryville-Lewis M. Ewing, President
Bank of Essex, Tappahannock-Earl R. Johnston, President
Bank of Fincastle, Fincastle-John F. Kilby, President
Bank of Floyd, Floyd-R. Leon Moore, President & CEO
Bank of Franklin, Franklin-Jerry R. Bryant, President and Cashier
Bank of Hampton Road, Chesapeake-Jack W. Gibson, President and CEO
Bank of Isle of Wight, Smithfield-Robert E. Spencer Jr., President
Bank of Lancaster, Kilmarnock-Austin L. Roberts, III, President and CEO
Bank of Loudoun, Leesburg-Kenneth L. Crovo, President and CEO
Bank of Marion, Marion-William D. Smith, President
Bank of McKenney, Inc., Mc Kenney-Richard M. Liles, President and CEO
Bank of Northumberland, Inc., Heathsville-Lewis R. Reynolds, President and COO
Bank of Rockbridge, Raphine-W. Lowrie Tucker, III, President
Bank of Southside Virginia, Carson-John H. Clements, Chairman and CEO
Bank of Suffolk, Suffolk-Harold U. Blythe, President and CEO
Bank of Sussex and Surry, Wakefield-D. Eugene Brittle, Executive Vice President and CEO
Bank of Tazewell County, Tazewell-Raymond E. Dodson, President
Bank of the Commonwealth, Norfolk-Edward J. Woodard, Jr., Chairman, President and CEO
Bank of the Potomac, Herndon-Thom F. Hanes, President and CEO
Bank of Tidewater, Virginia Beach-Elizabeth A. Duke, President
Bank of Waverly, Waverly-Glenn T. McCall, Executive Vice President and CEO
Bank Services of Virginia, Inc., Bassett-Worth H. Carter, Jr., President and Chairman
Benchmark Community Bank, Kenbridge-Ben L. Watson, III, President and CEO
Big Stone Gap Bank & Tr Co., Big Stone Gap-Kenneth L. Crank, Executive VP & CEO
Blue Grass Valley Bank, Blue Grass-Anthony E. Crane, Cashier and CEO
Blue Ridge Bank, Floyd-Peter Kessler, Vice President
Burke & Herbert Bank and Trust, Alexandria-C.S. Taylor Burke, Jr., Chairman and CEO
Central Fidelity Bank, Inc., Richmond-Carroll L. Saine, Chairman and CEO

Central Virginia Bank, Powhatan-Ralph Larry Lyons, President and CEO
Chesapeake National Bank, Kilmarnock-Douglas D. Monroe, Jr., Chairman, President and CEO
Citizens and Farmers Bank, West Point-Larry G. Dillon, President
Citizens Bank & Trust Co., Blackstone-J. A. Wilson, Jr., President
Citizens Bank of Tazewell, Tazewell-Monte K. Rife, Executive Vice President/CEO
Citizens Bank of Virginia, Arlington-Linwood C. Cotman, President and CEO
Commerce Bank, Virginia Beach-G. Robert Aston, Jr., President and CEO
Commerce Bank of Virginia, Richmond-Richard C. Huffman, President
Community Bank of Northern VA, Sterling-David P. Summers, President and CEO
Consolidated Bank & Trust Co., Richmond-Vernard W. Henley, Chairman, President and CEO
County Bank of Chesterfield, Midlothian-H.E. Richeson, President and CEO
Crestar Financial Corp., Richmond-Richard G. Tilghman, Chairman and CEO
Dickenson-Buchanan Bank, Haysi-Gaines C. Sutherland, Jr., President and CEO
Dominion Bank National Association, Roanoke-Warner N. Dalhouse, Chairman & CEO
F&M National Corp., Winchester, W.M. Feltner, Chairman and President
F&M Bank-Richmond, Richmond-James H. Atkinson, Jr., President and CEO
F&M Bank-Broadway, Broadway-Robert E. Driver, Senior Vice President
F&M Bank-Central Virginia, Charlottesville-Wayne L. Turner, President and CEO
F&M Bank-Massanutten, Harrisonburg-Wayne L. Smith, President and CEO
F&M Bank-Winchester, Winchester-Betty H. Carroll, President and CEO
Fairfax Bank & Trust Co., Fairfax-Charles E. Curtis, President
Farmers & Merchants Bank, Timberville-Dan B. Todd, Chairman
Farmers & Merchants Bank-ES, Onley-H.B. Rew, Jr., President
Farmers & Merchants Bank of Craig Co., New Castle-Jack W. Bostic, Jr., Exec. Vice President
Farmers & Merchants National Bank, Hamilton-Clyde C. Lamond, III, Chairman and CEO
Farmers & Merchants National Bank, Stanley-C. Gaylon Waters, Chief Executive Officer
Farmers & Miners Bank, Pennington Gap-Terry M. Estep, Executive Vice President & CEO
Farmers Bank, Windsor-Richard J. Holland, Sr., Chairman and CEO
Fauquier National Bank, Warrenton-C. Hunton Tiffany, President
First & Citizens Bank, Monterey-Delbert Rexrode, Jr., Vice President and Cashier
First American Bank, McLean-Fred L. Bollerer, Chairman and CEO
First Bank and Trust Co., Abingdon-William H. Hayter, President and CEO
First Century Bank, Wytheville-Jefferey L. Forlines, President
First Commercial Bank, Arlington-James B. Brockett, Chairman and President
First Commonwealth Bank, Wise-Sue Ellen Fleming, Executive Vice President and CEO
First Community Bank, Forest-John L. Wynne, President
First National Bank of Saltville, Saltville-James H. Campbell, President and CEO
First National Bank, Emporia-O. Wayne Hanks, President and CEO
First National Bank, Altavista-Robert H. Gilliam, Jr., President and CEO
First National Bank, Clifton Forge-George J. Kostel, Chairman and President
First National Bank, Christiansburg-Samuel H. Tollison, President
First National Bank of Ferrum, Ferrum-Larry A. Heaton, President/CEO
First National Bank of Rocky Mount, Rocky Mount-Worth Harris Carter, Jr., Chairman & Pres.
First National Bank of Stuart, Stuart-Jack E. Ward, Executive Vice President and CEO
First Sentinel Bank, Richlands-W. David Peters, President and CEO
First State Bank, Danville-Sylvesta L. Jennings, President
First Union Bank of Virginia, Vienna-Benjamin Jenkins, President & CEO
First Virginia Banks, Inc., Falls Church, Robert H. Zalokar, Chairman and CEO
First Virginia Bank-Commonwealth, Williamsburg-Jon A. Nystrom, President and CEO
First Virginia Bank-Mountain Empire, Wise-Larry L. Richardson, President and CEO
First Virginia Bank of Tidewater, Norfolk-James F. Babcock, Chairman and CEO
First Virginia Bank, Falls Church-Justin C. O'Donnell, President
First Virginia Bank of Augusta, Staunton-Miles F. P. Willett, President
First Virginia Bank-Central, Charlottesville-Edward S. Yates, President
First Virginia Bank-Colonial, Richmond-William H. McFaddin, President and CEO
First Virginia Bank-Highlands, Covington-Patrick H. Winston, Jr., President and CEO
First Virginia Bank-Piedmont, Lynchburg-Benjamin T. Corish, President and CEO
First Virginia Bank-Planters, Bridgewater-Donald E. McFall, President and CEO
First Virginia Bank-South Hill, South Hill-James H. Wells, President
First Virginia Bank-Southside, Farmville-John M. Lee, President & CEO
First Virginia Bank-Southwest, Roanoke-James N. Hinson, Jr., President and CEO
First Virginia Bank-Clinch Valley, Richlands-Michael J. Fircetz, President
First Virginia Bank-Franklin Co., Rocky Mount-Euell W. Naff, President
First Virginia Bank-Shen. Valley, Woodstock-Charles R. Cash, President
George Washington Nat. Bank, Alexandria-J. William Kilpatrick, President
Grayson National Bank, Independence-Carl J. Richardson, President
Grundy National Bank, Grundy-William B. Compton, Ex. Vice Pres. & CEO
Hallmark Bank & Trust Co., Springfield-Hugh W. Compton, President & CEO
Hanover Bank, Mechanicsville-Stafford M. White, President and CEO
Heritage Bank & Trust, Norfolk-Robert J. Keogh, President and CEO
Highlands Union Bank, Abingdon-Samuel L. Neese, Executive Vice President and CEO

Horizon Bank of Virginia, Fairfax-James N. Newsome, President and CEO
Independent Bank, Manassas-Gary R. English, President
Jefferson Bankshares, Inc., Charlottesville-Hovey S. Dabney, Chairman and CEO
King George State Bank, King George-Homer L. Hite, President
Lee Bank & Trust Company, Pennington Gap-Lewis G. Oatts, Executive Vice President
Marshall National Bk. & Tr. Co., Marshall-Donald R. Yowell, President and CEO
Middleburg National Bank, Middleburg-Joseph L. Boling, President
Miners & Merchants Bk. & Tr., Grundy-James G. Graham, President
Miners Exchange Bank, Coeburn-Charles R. Ward, President and CEO
National Bank of Blacksburg, Blacksburg-James G. Rakes, President
National Bank of Fredericksburg, Fredericksburg-Charles T. Lewis, President
NationsBank/Virginia, Richmond-Randolph W. McElroy, President
New Atlantic Bank, NA, Norfolk-Jesse E. Fleming, President
Northern Neck State Bank, Warsaw-E. Peyton Motley, President
Old Point National Bank, Hampton-Robert F. Shuford, Chairman and CEO
Pace American Bank, Lawrenceville-John E. Traylor, President and CEO
Page Valley National Bank, Luray-Leland F. Pittman, President
Patriot National Bank, Reston-Carroll C. Markley
Peninsula Trust Bank, Inc., Gloucester-William J. Farinholt, President/CEO
People's Bank, Inc., Honaker-Kenneth D. Hart, President and CEO
Peoples Bank of Danville, Danville-Worth Harris Carter, Jr., Chairman and President
Peoples Bank of Ewing, Ewing-Micki Yeary, Executive Vice President
Peoples Bank of Montross, Montross-William R. Crews, Jr., President and CEO
Peoples Bank of Virginia, Chesterfield-Quentin L. Corbett, President and CEO
Peoples National Bank of Warrenton, Warrenton-Mark C. Riley, President and CEO
Piedmont Trust Bank, Martinsville-Irving M. Groves, Jr., President
Planters Bank & Trust Co., Staunton-Harry V. Boney, Jr., President and CEO
Powell Valley National Bank, Jonesville-Lloyd C. Martin, Jr., Ex. Vice President and CEO
Premier Bank, Inc., Wytheville-Thomas G. Anders, President and CEO
Princess Anne Bank, Virginia Beach-J. Morgan Davis, President
Prosperity Bank & Trust Co., Springfield-Robert J. McDonough, President
Rappahannock National Bank, Washington-John R. Conry, Jr., Exec. Vice President and CEO
Regency Bank, Richmond-Herbert E. Marth, Jr., President and CEO
Resource Bank, Virginia Beach-Lawrence N. Smith, President and CEO
Richlands National Bank, Richlands-James M. Ratliff, President and CEO
Rockingham Heritage Bank, Harrisonburg-Bruce W. Thompson, President
Salem Bank & Trust, NA, Salem-Clark Owen, Jr., President and CEO
Second National Bank, Culpeper-W. Douglas Kyle, Jr., President
Security Bank Corporation, Manassas-Richard B. Green, President and CEO
Signet Banking Corporation, Richmond-Robert M. Freeman, Chairman and CEO
South Boston Bank, South Boston-Lonnie D. Powell, Vice President and Cashier
Southside Bank, Tappahannock, Thomas M. Boyd, Jr., President and CEO
State Bank of Remington, Remington-Larry B. Olinger, President
State Bank of the Alleghenies, Covington-Don E. Stone, Jr., President and CEO
Suburban Bank of Virginia, McLean-T. Allen Phillips, President and CEO
Tazewell National Bank, Tazewell-James R. Wheeling, President and CEO
The Bank of Northern Virginia, Arlington-Fred A. Burroughs, III, Chairman and CEO
The Business Bank, Vienna-Sheri C. Van Vranken, President
The CommonWealth Bank, Richmond-J.E. Causey Davis, President and CEO
The Community Bank, Petersburg-Nathan S. Jones, III, President and CEO
The Eastville Bank, Eastville-Robert L. Simpson, President
The Farmers Bank, Appomattox-James J. Pugh, Jr., President/CEO
The First National Bank, Strasburg-Ronald F. Miller, President
The George Mason Bank, Fairfax-Marshall H. Groom, Chairman/CEO
The Heritage Bank, McLean-Harold C. Rauner, President
The Marathon Bank, Winchester-Donald L. Unger, President and CEO
The Marine Bank, Chincoteague-Joe T. Hutcherson, Executive Vice President
The Riggs National Bank of Virginia, Merrifield-Robert C. Roane, President & Director
Tysons National Bank, Vienna-Terrie G. Spiro, President and CEO
Union Bank and Trust Co., Bowling Green-G. William Beale, President and CEO
Virginia Bank & Trust Co., Danville-D.C. Hastings, Jr., President and CEO
Virginia Banker's Bank, Richmond-Raymond B. Cavedo, Jr., President
Virginia Commerce Bank, NA, Arlington-Conley Ricker, President
Virginia Community Bank, Louisa-A. Pierce Stone, President
Virginia Heartland Bank, Fredericksburg-William B. Young, Chairman of the Board & CEO

9

Bank Assets in Virginia

Assets of Virginia banks (year end):

1960	$3.642 billion	
1970	7.347 billion	
1980	20.838 billion	
1985	43.705 billion	
1986	51.264 billion	
1987	56.174 billion	
1988	61.553 billion	
1989	67.695 billion	
1990	69.613 billion	
1992	68.867 billion	(9/22/92)

Total number of banks	171
Total number of BHCs	19
Total assets of BHCs	$53.4 billion
Total number of banking offices	2,098
Total banking assets per capital	$10,956
Total people per banking office	2,996

10

100th Anniversary Task Force

THE VBA 100TH ANNIVERSAY TASK FORCE has been aggressive in its activity to celebrate the first century of the Association.

The members are:

S. Joseph Ward, Chairman, Signet Bank (retired); Gloria J. Abel, Commerce Bank; Douglas M. Church, Jr., First Virginia Banks, Inc.; John H. Clements, Bank of Southside Virginia; William R. Crews, Jr., Peoples Bank of Montross; Richard J. Holland, The Farmers Bank; Monte L. Layman, Jefferson National Bank; Judith Snyderman, Signet Bank; H.B. Rew, Jr., Farmers & Merchants Bank-Eastern Shore; Jean A. Segner, Central Fidelity Bank; William D. Smith,

Bank of Marion; Paul H. Geithner, Jr., and Irmy Geithner, First Virginia Banks, Inc.

The Task Force prepared many projects and commemorative items promoting the 100th anniversary.

In the early 1900s, the Virginia Bankers Association adapted the seal shown below to appear on its publications, etc.

The 100th Anniversary Task Force has adopted the following logo to go forward into the second 100 years.

This benchmark event reinforces the role of banking in the Old Dominion and underlines the legacy of men and women who dedicated themselves to the growth and service of Virginia. It also shows that history is timeless.

President

Paul H. Geithner, Jr.
VBA President 1992-93

President-Elect

Vern W. Henley
VBA President—1993-94

Clements

Freeman

Monroe

Shumadine

Appropriate for the 100th Anniversary Convention will be a panel on "Perspectives of the Past: Looking Towards the Future," Panelists will be four former Presidents of the VBA, John H. Clements, Carson; Robert M. Freeman, Richmond; Douglas D. Monroe, Jr., Kilmarnock; and William F. Shumadine, Richmond. Noted writer and speaker Arnold G. Danielson will serve as moderator for the panel.

Index